Book A
Teacher's Guide and Answer Key

VOCABULARY
FROM
CLASSICAL ROOTS

Norma Fifer ▼ Nancy Flowers

EDUCATORS PUBLISHING SERVICE
Cambridge and Toronto

Editors: Stacey L. Nichols, Jen Noon
Managing Editor: Sheila Neylon

Printed in Benton Harbor, MI, in June 2011
ISBN 978-0-8388-0860-3

7 8 9 10 11 PPG 15 14 13 12 11

Contents

Introduction

Words derived from Greek and Latin roots account for about 60 percent of the English language. By learning the most common roots and frequently used affixes, students can unlock the meanings of thousands of words. *Vocabulary from Classical Roots* can help students learn these roots and prefixes so that they succeed not only with this series, but also with new words they encounter in daily life. The Teacher's Guide is a powerful educational tool that complements, extends, and enriches the series.

The guide provides scaffolding for individual learning needs. The activities in the guide help students access prior knowledge and make connections to new learning, while also providing students with additional experience using key words.

The activities featured in this Teacher's Guide are flexible and varied. Many can be adapted to suit whole-class, small-group, or independent learning situations with different instruction schedules. A variety of written and oral word games provides students more practice with familiar and key vocabulary words from the lessons. These games include limericks and other poems; rhyming riddles; dictionary games; anagrams; coded messages; jokes and puns; and crossword puzzles.

Lesson Format

Every lesson has the following format:

Literary and Historical References
INTRODUCE Lesson
PREVIEW Familiar Words
PRESENT Key Words
GUIDE Practice
Key Word Activity Master
ASSIGN Exercises
REVIEW Lessons (after every two lessons)
SELECT Review Exercises (after every two lessons)

Literary and Historical References

Many of the illustrative sentences refer to literary works or historical events. For your convenience, a list of the references is included at the start of each lesson. You may wish to discuss them with your students when the reference appears in a sentence.

INTRODUCE Lesson

Introduce or review the theme of each lesson pair by displaying, reading, and translating the opening quotation for each lesson and connecting the quote to the lesson content.

PREVIEW Familiar Words

Help students make connections with familiar words that have the same roots as the new words they will be learning about in the lesson. The goal of the preview section is to access students' prior knowledge in order to build a context for learning new, related words.

PRESENT Key Words

Display the roots from the lesson and give their meanings. Read the list of new key words chorally from the student book. Key words are presented through discussion of pronunciation, definition and connection to the root, example sentences, parts of speech, and word forms. Special *Nota Bene* sections are discussed in detail.

GUIDE Practice

Participate with students in a short, interactive activity that reinforces the meanings of the key words.

Key Word Activity Master

Further reinforce the meanings of the key words. It can be completed as an independent, small-group, or whole-class activity. There is one reproducible master for each lesson; they are all located at the end of the Teacher's Guide.

ASSIGN Exercises

Assign student book exercises. Suggestions for how to complete these exercises can be found on page x.

REVIEW Lessons

Review words from the previous two lessons in this interactive activity.

SELECT Review Exercises

Assign student book review exercises. Suggestions for how to complete these exercises can be found on page x.

Additional Vocabulary Games and Activities

Here are some suggestions for reinforcement and review.

Scavenger Hunt

Ask members of competing teams where they would go to find a specific person or object indicated by a key word from the lesson. For example, "Where in the school would you go to find a *copious* supply of pencils?" Possible answer: the supply closet.

Pantomime/Charades

Have students act out a key word. The rest of the students try to guess the correct word.

Quick on the Draw/Pictorial Charades

Divide students into two teams. One student from each team sketches a picture of a target word while his or her teammates try to guess what word is being drawn. The first team to guess correctly gets a point.

Creating Words

Have students create new words using one or more of the roots from the lesson. Students can also provide a definition, an illustrative sentence, and/or an illustration of the word. For example, a student who studied the roots *micro* (meaning "small") and *bovis* (meaning "cow") might create the word *microbovis*, define it as "a really tiny breed of cattle," and draw a picture of a tiny cow. Have the students display their created words for the rest of the class.

Root Bingo

To review several lessons, create a number of different bingo boards (3x3 or 5x5 grid), filling in the boxes with Greek and Latin roots from the various lessons. Give each student a board and provide bingo chips or other markers. Write the key words and their definitions on cards, then put them in a container. Pull out a card, and read the word and the definition. Students place a bingo chip on the root from which that word derives.

Flashcards

Have students write the key word on the front of a note card and the definition on the back. Students can review these words independently or with a partner.

Sorts

Using flashcards, students sort words by common roots and then state the definition of each word.

Additional Word-Learning Strategies and Activities

When students will benefit from a more in-depth exploration of a vocabulary word, the following word-learning strategies and activities may be helpful. These strategies can be especially useful for content-area terminology—vocabulary words with connections to social studies, science, or math.

Root Webs

A root web can help students identify origins and meanings that are common to a group of words. Display the root in the middle of the web and discuss its meaning. Complete the rest of the web with words that include that root. This can include different forms of the same word. Discuss definitions and relationship of the word to the root. Also, clarify confusing words that may appear to include the root but have other origins; for example, the word "tricky" has the letters *t, r,* and *i* at the beginning but does not relate to the number three.

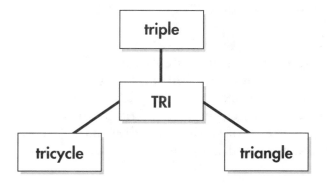

Comparing and Contrasting Words or Concepts with Venn Diagrams

A Venn diagram is especially useful in helping students understand the relationship among content area concepts through comparison and contrast. For example, the following Venn diagram can help show the differences and similarities between a *monarch* and a *magnate*. The overlap of the circles shows what qualities are shared.

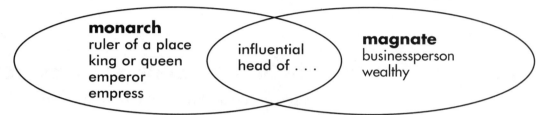

Concept of Definition Maps

Concept of Definition maps are visual displays that show the common components of a dictionary definition. Students can use context, prior knowledge, and dictionaries to fill in the map as they answer the following questions:

- *What is it?*
- *What is it like?*
- *What are some specific examples of the word?*
- *What are some specific nonexamples of the word?*

Independently or in groups, students fill in the map then use the information on the map to write a definition of the key word. The following map clarifies the meaning of the word *monarch*.

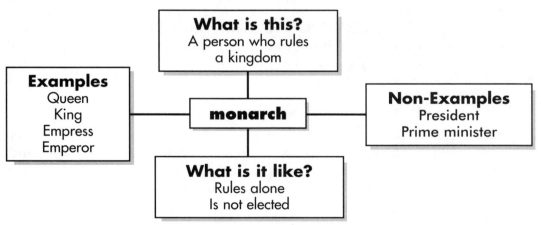

Students then use the map to write a definition for the word. For example, *A monarch is a ruler of a kingdom or empire. A monarch rules alone and is not elected by people. Some kinds of monarchs are queens, kings, and emperors.*

Word Building and Parts of Speech

Ask students to add an array of affixes to word roots to create long words. For example, ask students to create as many words as they can by combining the root *vis* with the affixes *-ible, in-,* and *-ity.* Then have students use the dictionary to determine each word's part of speech. For more of a challenge, have students mix and match word parts. For example, ask students what real words they can make with the morphemes *vise, pro-, -gress, -ion, re-.* Then have students use the dictionary to determine each word's part of speech.

Suggestions For Completing Student Book Exercises

The following directions can provide additional help to students.

General Suggestions

For each exercise, read the directions and underline, circle, or highlight important words (*synonym, antonym, used incorrectly, most appropriate*) that indicate how to complete the exercise.

Exercise A: Synonyms and Antonyms

Synonyms: When the directions say to circle the letter of the word or phrase MOST NEARLY THE SAME as the word in boldfaced type, substitute each suggested answer for the boldfaced word to see if that answer makes sense in that phrase. Pay attention to any context clues in the phrase that may help to choose the correct word. Cross out any answers that do not make sense. Ask whether the chosen word has the same or nearly the same meaning as the boldfaced word. Check that the chosen word is the same part of speech (such as noun, verb, adjective).

Antonyms: When the directions say to circle the letter of the word or phrase MOST NEARLY THE OPPOSITE to the word in boldfaced type, take the boldfaced word out of the sentence. Ask whether the chosen word has the opposite or nearly the opposite meaning to the boldfaced word. Cross out any answers that do not make sense.

Exercise B: Incorrect Usage

Read each sentence, paying particular attention to context clues. Consult the definition of the word as necessary, paying particular attention to multiple meanings. Find the one sentence in which the boldfaced key word is not used properly. If completing this in class, discuss answers with partners or in small groups.

Exercise C: Fill-in-the-Blank

Read the entire sentence and highlight any context clues. Look at the key words, and determine which ones might relate to the context clues. Rule out any obvious incorrect answers. Then substitute possible answers for the blank and read the sentence to decide which word fits best.

Review Exercises

Analogies

Analogies in *Vocabulary from Classical Roots* usually focus on discovering the relationship between two given roots or words. Sometimes the roots or words provided are synonyms or antonyms. Sometimes a key word and a root are provided. The first step in solving analogies is to know what each root or word means. Look back at the definitions in the beginning of the lesson. If the relationship is not immediately clear, it helps to create a sentence that describes the relationship between the given word pair. Use that same sentence to solve the other half of the analogy. Modify the relationship sentence as needed in order to create a sentence that will work in both pairs of words.

Writing or Discussion Activities

Exercises can be completed individually, in pairs, or small groups. If done in pairs, each group of students should have its own question and should present its answers in a whole-group discussion.

Scheduling Instruction in Your Classroom

The organization of the lessons can accommodate a variety of instructional schedules. Some of the shorter activities can be combined to create longer lessons. Other activities can be assigned as homework according to class schedule and individual needs. This table of approximate completion times will help you manage your vocabulary instruction schedule.

	Description	Approximate completion time	Need student book?
1.	**INTRODUCE Lesson X**	5 minutes	No
2.	**PREVIEW Familiar Words**	10-15 minutes	No
3.	**PRESENT Key Words**	20 minutes	Yes
4.	**GUIDE Practice**	15 minutes	Optional
5.	**Key Word Activity Master***	15 minutes	Optional
6.	**ASSIGN Exercises***	30 minutes	Yes
7.	**REVIEW Lessons X and X**	15 minutes	Optional
8.	**SELECT Review Exercises**	15 minutes	Yes

* Can be assigned as homework

Keep in mind that if you will be using the *Vocabulary from Classical Roots* tests, they need to be incorporated into your instructional schedule.

LESSON 1

Literary and Historical References

2. monarch   Queen Victoria ruled the British Empire from 1837–1901, a period of peace and prosperity.

3. monogram   Napoleon Bonaparte (1769–1821) ruled France as the self-styled "Emperor of the French" from 1804 to 1815.

Exercise 1B, 1a   In 1918, following the defeat of the German Empire in World War I, Kaiser Wilhelm II (1859–1941) was deposed and the Weimar Republic, a constitutional democracy, was established to rule Germany.

Exercise 1B, 1c   Born in 1929, Queen Elizabeth II has ruled as constitutional monarch of Great Britain since 1952.

Exercise 1B, 2a   In *The Belle of Amherst*, a dramatic performance based on the life and poetry of Emily Dickinson (1830–1886), a single actor portrays the poet, who spent her life in Amherst, Massachusetts.

Exercise 1B, 2d   Two critical scenes between the two lovers immortalized in Shakespeare's play *Romeo and Juliet* take place on the balcony outside Juliet's bedroom.

Exercise 1B, 3a   In *1984*, George Orwell (1903–1950) depicts a future world in which individual liberties are restricted by a totalitarian state, personified by the ever-watching Big Brother.

Exercise 1B, 3b   The origins and purpose of Stonehenge, the circle of monoliths that stand on the Salisbury Plain of southern England, have invited centuries of speculation.

Exercise 1B, 6b   The neighboring countries of Poland, Latvia, and Estonia, along with Lithuania, are often referred to as Baltic states.

Exercise 1C, 1   Queen Lydia Kamekeha Liliuokalani (1838–1917) ruled the Hawaiian Islands from 1891 to 1893.

Exercise 1C, 2   In the Greek epic *The Odyssey*, its hero Odysseus recounts his experiences during warfare and his lengthy travels in a "flashback" during a banquet at the court of King Alcinous of Phaeacia.

INTRODUCE Lesson 1

(Book A, page 3)

Tell students that the theme of Lessons 1 and 2 is "Numbers."
Display, read, and translate the opening quotation from Lesson 1: *E pluribus unum.* "One from many."

- Ask students if anyone knows where this Latin phrase can be found. Hint: It is presented on something everyone uses. Look on the backs of quarters, dimes, nickels, and pennies. It is the motto of the United States—one country from many states.
- Point out that *unus* is a Latin root that means "one," and it is one of the roots presented in Lesson 1. It ties with the "Numbers" theme.

PREVIEW Familiar Words

(Book A, pages 4–6)

monorail, monotonous, unicycle, unique, double, bicycle

ACTIVITY 1: *monos*

Display the familiar words *monorail* and *monotonous*. Read them orally, pointing at each one, and then chorally with the class. Underline *mono* in each word.

Ask students the following questions:

- What is a *monorail*? (If nobody volunteers the correct answer, have a student use the dictionary.)
- What makes a *monorail* different from other trains or tracks? (one rail or track)
- What do you think *mono* might mean, since a monorail has **one** rail or track? (one)
- Tell students that you will demonstrate a *monotonous* tone of voice. (Speak for a few moments in a flat, dull, unchanging voice with no variety in pitch. Use just one tone.) Ask them if your voice was lively with many different tones. (no) How many tones do they hear in a *monotonous* voice? (just one)

Ask: What is the shared meaning for *mono* in these words? (one)

ACTIVITY 2: *unus, duo, bi*

Display the familiar words *unicycle, unique, double,* and *bicycle.* Read them orally, pointing at each one, and then chorally with the class. Underline *uni* in the first two words, and *dou* and *bi* in the last two.

Ask students the following questions:

- How many wheels are there on a *unicycle*? (one)
- How many are there on a *bicycle*? (two)
- How many meat patties in a *double* burger? (two)
- Whatever is *unique* is "one of a kind." Are jeans *unique* clothing? (no) Does the President of the United States have a *unique* job? (yes)

Ask: What shared meaning for *uni* is in the words *unicycle* and *unique*? (one)

Ask: What do a bicycle and a double burger have in common? (both contain two of something)

Review: The familiar words indicate that *monos* and *unus* suggest "one," and *duo* and *bi* suggest "two."

PRESENT Key Words

(Book A, pages 3–6)

Display the Lesson 1 Greek and Latin roots and review their meanings:

- the Greek root *monos* (*mono*), meaning "one"
- the Latin root *unus* (*un*), meaning "one"
- the Latin root *duo* (*du*), meaning "two" and *duplex* (*du*), meaning "twofold"
- the Latin root *bi*, meaning "two"

Have students read the key words chorally: *bilateral, bipartisan, bisect, duplex, duplicate, monarch, monogram, monolith, monologue, monopoly, unanimous, unilateral.*

Present each of the key words by discussing the following:

- pronunciation
- definitions/connections to the root
- sentences
- parts of speech
- word forms

The *Nota Bene* on page 5 presents interesting material on the derivation from *unus* of *unicorn, onion, inch,* and *ounce.*

GUIDE Practice

ACTIVITY 1

Words Connected by the Meaning "One": *monos* and *unus*

Display the key words in groups that show their similarities. Work first with the words connected by the meaning "one." Shorten and simplify the definitions you display, as shown below, to give students an element of meaning they can grasp quickly, hang on to, and remember for each word.

> one ruler
>
> one letter
>
> one large stone
>
> one speaker
>
> one owner
>
> all for one
>
> one-sided

Read the preceding words and short definitions chorally with students. Allow them a minute or two to study the definitions silently. Then erase the definitions, leaving just the key words. Read aloud these seven clues, and have students write the word they associate with each clue.

Clue	Answer
1. initials embroidered on towels	*monogram*
2. real estate buying game	*monopoly*
3. lecture from a parent	*monologue*
4. king or queen	*monarch*
5. everybody voting for the same candidate	*unanimous*
6. huge slab of rock	*monolith*
7. decisions by one political party	*unilateral*

ACTIVITY 2

Words Connected by the Meaning "Two": *duo, duplex, bi*

Display the words connected by the meaning "two" with short definitions, as shown below.

duplex	two-family house	*bilateral*	two sided
duplicate	two copies	*bipartisan*	two political parties
		bisect	cut in two

Proceed through the choral reading, silent studying, and erasing of the preceding short definitions, as you did with the "one" words. Then read aloud these five clues for the "two" words, and have students write the word they associate with each clue.

Clue	**Answer**
1. Democrats and Republicans	*bipartisan*
2. kitchens back to back	*duplex*
3. copying machine	*duplicate*
4. dividing into parts	*bisect*
5. treaty benefiting both countries	*bilateral*

LESSON 1 Key Word Activity Master (see page 85)

Answers:

1. B
2. D
3. A
4. C

5–8. (in any order) unicycle, unilateral, bicycle, bilateral

9. unilateral
10. unicycle
11. bilateral
12. bicycle
13. monarch
14. unanimous
15. bipartisan
16. duplex
17. duplicate
18. monopolize

ASSIGN Exercises

(Book A, pages 6–8)

LESSON 2

Literary and Historical References

1. trilogy
Oxford philologist John Ronald Reuel Tolkien (1892–1973) wrote fantasy adventure novels, including *The Lord of the Rings*, that incorporate the heroic material drawn from his academic studies.

3. triumvirate
Immediately following the fall of Julius Caesar in 44 B.C., power was jointly held by Mark Antony, Augustus Caesar, and Lepidus; by 30 B.C. Augustus had defeated the other two and established himself as the first Roman emperor.

9. bicentennial
The home of French rulers until the seventeenth century, the Louvre is now the principal art museum of Paris; its wing of glass and steel was the subject of much controversy when it opened in 1988 during the bicentennial celebrations of the French Revolution.

Exercise 2C, 1
Set in the mythical kingdom of Earthsea, *The Earthsea Trilogy* by Ursula K. LeGuin (b. 1929) recounts the adventures of a young boy who must learn to use his magical powers wisely.

INTRODUCE Lesson 2

(Book A, page 9)

Remind students that the theme of Lessons 1 and 2 is "Numbers."
Display, read, and translate the opening quotation from Lesson 2: *Gallia est omnis divisa in partes tres.* "All Gaul is divided into three parts."

- Ask students if anyone has heard of the great Roman leader, Julius Caesar, who lived about 2,000 years ago. Tell them he conquered Gaul (now France), and divided the conquered territory into three parts. If you wish, ask students to find more information about Caesar on the Internet or in the encyclopedia.

- Point out that *tres* is the last word in the Latin quotation that opens this lesson. *Tres* is also a Latin root that means "three," and it is one of the roots covered in Lesson 2. It ties with the "Numbers" theme.

PREVIEW Familiar Words

(Book A, pages 9–11)

trio, triplet, quadruplet, quarter, century, centipede

ACTIVITY 1: *tri*

Display the familiar words *trio* and *triplet*. Read them orally, pointing at each one, and then chorally with the class. Underline *tri* in each word.

Ask students the following questions:

- Have a student draw stick-figure *triplets* on the board. How many people are there? (three)
- How many singers in a *trio*? (three)

Ask: What is the shared meaning for *tri* in these words? (three)

ACTIVITY 2: *quartus* and *quatuor*

Display the familiar words *quarter* and *quadruplets*. Read them orally, pointing at each one, and then chorally with the class.

Ask students the following questions:

- Have a student draw *quadruplets* on the board. How many people are there? (four)
- How many *quarters* are there in a dollar? (four)

Ask: What is the shared meaning in these words? (four)

ACTIVITY 3: *centum*

Display the familiar words *century* and *centipede*. Read them orally, pointing at each one, and then chorally with the class. Underline *cent* in each word.

Ask students the following questions:

- Ask how many years in a *century*. (one hundred)
- How many legs on a *centipede*? (one hundred)

Ask: What is the shared meaning for *cent* in these words? (one hundred)

Review: The familiar words indicate that *tri* suggests "three," *quar* and *quat* (or *quad*) suggest "four," and *cent* suggests "one hundred."

PRESENT Key Words

(Book A, pages 9–12)

Display the Lesson 2 Greek and Latin roots and review their meanings:

- the Greek root *tri* and the Latin root *tres* (*tri*), meaning "three"
- the Latin roots *quartus* (*quad, quar, quat*), meaning "fourth" and *quatuor* (*quad, quar, quat*), meaning "four"
- the Latin root *decem* (*deca, deci*), meaning "ten"
- the Latin root *centum* (*cent*), meaning "hundred"

Have students read the key words chorally: *bicentennial, centenary, centigrade, decathlon, decimate, quadrant, quartet, quatrain, trilogy, trisect, triumvirate.*

Present each of the key words by discussing the following:

- pronunciation
- definitions/connections to the root
- sentences
- parts of speech
- word forms

The *Nota Bene* on page 10 extends the "Numbers" theme by presenting roots that relate to the numbers five through nine.

GUIDE Practice

ACTIVITY 1: True or False

Have students print TRUE on a piece of green paper, and FALSE on a piece of red paper. Tell them to listen to each key word and sentence that you read aloud, decide whether the sentence is true or false, and mentally select the proper paper.

Then, on a signal from you, they should close their eyes and hold up either TRUE (green paper) or FALSE (red paper). This way, you can prevent copycat answering, and you can tell at a glance which students are correct and incorrect.

1.	*Bicentennial.*	The year 1976 was the *bicentennial* of 1776.	true
2.	*Centigrade.*	Water boils at one hundred degrees *centigrade*.	true
3.	*Quartet.*	There are three singers in a *quartet*.	false
4.	*Quatrain.*	A *quatrain* is four lines long.	true
5.	*Decathlon.*	A *decathlon* includes ten athletic events.	true
6.	*Quadrant.*	A *quadrant* is one fifth of a circle.	false
7.	*Trilogy.*	A *trilogy* ends with the third book.	true
8.	*Centenary.*	The *centenary* celebration of 1920 will be in 2020.	true
9.	*Trisect.*	To *trisect* is to divide in half.	false
10.	*Triumvirate.*	Three governors formed a *triumvirate*.	true
11.	*Decimated.*	Everyone recovered when measles *decimated* the town.	false

LESSON 2 Key Word Activity Master (see page 86)

Answers:

1. 3
2. 4
3. 100
4. 3
5. 100
6. decathlon
7. quadrant
8. trisect
9. decimate
10. centigrade
11. quatrain
12. B
13. A
14. D
15. C
16. E

ASSIGN Exercises

(Book A, pages 12–13)

REVIEW Lessons 1 and 2

Write the numbers 1, 2, 3, 4, 10, and 100 on the board. Divide the class into four teams. Give each team chalk of a different color. Tell students to keep their books open for this activity, and look back at the key words in Lessons 1 and 2 (pages 3–13).

Have team members take turns going to the board, writing a key word under the corresponding number (1, 2, 3, 4, 10, or 100), and using the word correctly in an oral sentence. The team with the most words in its color wins.

SELECT Review Exercises

(Book A, pages 14–15)

LESSON 3

Literary and Historical References

1. pandemonium In *Julius Caesar*, one of Shakespeare's Roman plays, the increasingly arrogant Caesar ignores warnings that the ides of March (the fifteenth) will bring danger to him, and he is stabbed by a group of conspirators in the Senate.

3. omnipotent Lacking either military power or centralized authority, the Celtic tribes inhabiting Britain in the first century B.C. were easily conquered by the invading Roman army led by Julius Caesar.

8. totalitarian Winner of a power struggle following the Russian Revolution of 1917, Joseph Stalin (1879–1953) held absolute authority in the Soviet Union until his death.

9. cloister Transmitted by lice and fleas from infected rats, epidemics of bubonic plague, known also as the Black Plague or Black Death, swept across Europe during the late Middle Ages.

Exercise 3B, 4b The animals stories and illustrations of Beatrix Potter (1866–1943) such as *The Tale of Peter Rabbit* and *The Tale of Mrs. Tittlemouse* are classics of children's literature.

Exercise 3C, 1 Since its development in the 1940s by Scottish biologist Alexander Fleming (1881–1955), penicillin has been the major drug used for treatment of infectious disease.

Exercise 3C, 2 Despite the objections of the Barrett family that Elizabeth could never marry, English poets Elizabeth Barrett Browning (1806–1861) and Robert Browning (1812–1889) eloped to Italy and raised a family there.

Exercise 3C, 3 A teenaged survivor of the concentration camp at Auschwitz, Elie Wiesel (b. 1928) has written extensively about the Holocaust.

Exercise 3C, 4 Montezuma II (1480?–1520), the last Aztec emperor of Mexico, was defeated by the Spanish conquistadores led by Hernando Cortes.

INTRODUCE Lesson 3

(Book A, page 16)

Tell students that the theme of Lessons 3 and 4 is "All or Nothing."

Display, read, and translate the opening quotation from Lesson 3: *Omni corpus mutabile est.* "Every object is subject to change."

- Ask students to restate the quotation in their own words. (possible answers: Everything changes. My bike is an object, and it is subject to changes like rust, flat tires, and broken spokes.)
- Point out that *omnis* is a Latin root that means "all." The Latin quotation for this lesson starts with the word *omni*, which is a form of *omnis*, meaning "all" or "every." It ties with the "All or Nothing" theme.

PREVIEW Familiar Words

(Book A, page 18)

total, totally, close, include, exclude

ACTIVITY 1: *totus*

Display the familiar words *total* and *totally*. Read them orally, pointing at each one, and then chorally with the class. Underline *tot* in each word.

Ask students the following questions:

- When you add numbers you get a sum. Which familiar word is a synonym of "sum"? (Total. The *total* is the "whole" amount.)
- Suppose you were caught in a downpour and got *totally* drenched. Would you be wet from head to toe? (Yes, the "whole" of you would be wet.)

Ask: What is the shared meaning for *tot* in these words? (whole)

ACTIVITY 2: *claudo*

Display the familiar words, *close, include,* and *exclude.* Read them orally, pointing at each one, and then chorally with the class. Underline the letters *clo* in *close,* and *clu* in *include* and *exclude.*

Ask students the following questions:

- Can you restate the sentence, "Close the door," using another word for *close*? (Shut the door.)
- Suppose a person is shut out from membership in a club. Which familiar word means "shut out"? (*excluded*)
- If you *include* someone in a circle, you close that person in. What do you do when you *exclude* someone? (You close, or shut, that person out.)

Ask: What is the shared meaning for *clo* and *clu* in the words? (close)

Review: The familiar words indicate that *tot* suggests "whole," and *clo* and *clu* suggest "close."

PRESENT Key Words

(Book A, pages 16–18)

Display the Lesson 3 Greek and Latin roots and review their meanings:

- the Greek root *pan,* meaning "all"
- the Latin root *omnis,* meaning "all"
- the Greek root *holos,* meaning "whole"
- the Latin root *totus,* meaning "whole"
- the Latin root *claudo, claudere, clausi, clausum (clo, clu),* meaning "to close"

Have students read the key words chorally: *catholic, cloister, holocaust, omnipotent, omnipresent, omnivorous, panacea, pandemonium, preclude, recluse, totalitarian.*

Present each of the key words by discussing the following:

- pronunciation
- definitions/connections to the root
- sentences
- parts of speech
- word forms

GUIDE Practice

ACTIVITY 1: Sound-meaning connection: *holos, totus*

Display the key words *holocaust, totalitarian, omnipresent* and *omnipotent.* Point out the sound-meaning connection between the roots and their derivatives, as follows:

- The root *holos* in *holocaust* sounds like and means "whole." In a *holocaust,* everything is wholly destroyed. Now apply the sound-meaning connection in *holos* to an unknown word. Do you think *holistic* medicine treats one part of the body or the whole person? (the whole person)
- The root *totus* in the word *totalitarian* sounds like and means "total." In a totalitarian government, one person has total control. Is the Canadian government *totalitarian*? (no)

ACTIVITY 2: Other connections: *pan, omnis* and *holos, claudo*

Display the remaining key words: *pandemonium, panacea, omnivorous, omnipotent, catholic, cloister, preclude, recluse.* Give students a minute or two to review the material on pages 16–19 of the Book A. As you read aloud each of the short connections or definitions below, have students respond orally with the correct key word.

1. cure-all   (*panacea*)
2. all foods   (*omnivorous*)
3. closed-in place   (*cloister*)
4. all powerful   (*omnipotent*)
5. closed-in person   (*recluse*)
6. all in an uproar   (*pandemonium*)
7. make it not happen   (*preclude*)
8. universal   (*catholic*)

Lesson 3 Key Word Activity Master (see page 87)

Answers:

1. B
2. A
3. D
4. C
5. F
6. E
7. total
8. present
9. close
10. potent
11. omnivorous
12. holocaust
13. preclude
14. catholic

ASSIGN Exercises

(Book A, pages 19–21)

LESSON 4

Literary and Historical References

3. annihilate

In 1938 American actor Orson Welles (1915–1985) broadcast a radio adaptation of H.G. Wells's (1866–1946) novel *The War of the Worlds* that created panic among listeners who believed it was a report of an actual Martian invasion.

5. negate

With his famous 1492 voyage that first brought Europeans to what is now called America, Christopher Columbus (1451–1506) established that ships sailing westward would not fall off the edge of the world.

8. vanity

Spanish artist Francisco José de Goya y Lucientes (1746–1828) is famous for his uncompromising portraits of the Spanish nobility as well as for his political paintings.

Exercise 4B, 1a

The literary reputation of English poet John Donne (1573–1631) rests on his erotic early poetry as well as his later holy sonnets and sermons.

Exercise 4B, 2a

Although she chose never to marry, the English Queen Elizabeth I (1533–1603) was greatly influenced by a succession of male favorites who cultivated the monarch's vanity.

Exercise 4B, 2b

In *Pilgrim's Progress,* the allegorical tale of salvation by Puritan John Bunyan (1628–1688), the hero Christian must overcome many obstacles and temptations, such as the bazaar of Vanity Fair, on his journey to Heaven.

Exercise 4B, 3b

Because Russian nihilists of the 1860s and 1870s denied established authority such as the church and the monarchy and advocated acts of violence against these institutions, they were actively suppressed by the Czars, especially Nicholas II (1868–1918).

Exercise 4B, 4a

Nicolaus Copernicus (1473–1543) was the first scientist to advance the heliocentric model of the solar system.

Exercise 4C, 7

Italian educator Maria Montessori (1870–1952) established a method of early childhood education that stresses the child's own initiative in learning.

INTRODUCE Lesson 4

(Book A, page 21)

Remind students that the theme of Lessons 3 and 4 is "All or Nothing."

Display, read, and translate the opening quotation from Lesson 4: *Humani nihil a me alienum puto.* "I think nothing human is alien to me."

- Ask students to try to rephrase the quotation in their own words. (possible answers: I am a neighbor to everyone else in our global village. I have something in common with all other human beings.)
- Point out the word *nihil* in the Latin quotation. Explain that *nihil* is also a Latin root that means "nothing," and it is one of the roots covered in Lesson 4. It ties with the "All or Nothing" theme.

PREVIEW Familiar Words

(Book A, pages 22–23)

nil, deny, negative, avoid, vain, void

ACTIVITY 1: *nihil, nego*

Display the familiar words *nil, deny,* and *negative.* Read them orally, pointing at each one, and then chorally with the class.

Ask students the following questions:

- If your allowance is *nil,* are you rich?   (no)
- If you *deny* a request for help, do you say *yes* or *no?* (no)
- If you feel *negative,* are you in a good mood?   (no)

Ask: The theme of this chapter is "All or Nothing." With which part of that theme are the words *nil, deny,* and *negative* connected? (nothing)

ACTIVITY 2: *vanus* and *vacuus*

Display the familiar words *avoid, vacuum,* and *evacuate.* Read them orally, pointing at each one, and then chorally with the class.

Ask students the following questions:

- Is a *void* full or empty? (empty)
- Can you use a *vacuum* to empty your carpet of dirt? (yes)
- After a room is *evacuated,* is it full of people or empty? (empty)

Ask: What is the shared meaning in these words? (empty)

PRESENT Key Words

(Book A, pages 21–23)

Display the Lesson 4 Latin roots and review their meanings:

- the Latin root *incipio, incipere, incepi, inceptum* (*incip*), meaning "to begin"
- the Latin root *nihil*, meaning "nothing"
- the Latin root *nego, negare, negivi, negatum* (*neg*), meaning "to deny"
- the Latin roots *vanus* (*van*) and *vacuus* (*vac, vacu*), meaning "empty"
- the Latin roots *aperio, aperire, aperui, apertum* (*aper*), meaning "to open"

Have students read the key words chorally: *annihilate, aperture, inception, incipient, negate, nihilism, overt, renegade, vacuous, vanity, vaunt.*

Present each of the key words by discussing the following:

- pronunciation
- definitions/connections to the root
- sentences
- parts of speech
- word forms

GUIDE Practice

ACTIVITY 1: The key words related to the meaning "nothing"

Display these key words: *annihilate, negate, nihilism, renegade, vacuous.*

Explain that they are all connected with the "nothing" part of this lesson's theme, but in different ways. Read aloud these nothing-related clues, and have students respond orally with the best key word.

1. belief in nothing   (*nihilism*)
2. person with loyalty to nothing   (*renegade*)
3. destroy, reduce to nothing   (*annihilate*)
4. deny, declare to be nothing   (*negate*)
5. nothing inside, empty   (*vacuous*)

ACTIVITY 2: Taking a "true-false" stand

Display these key words: *aperture, inception, incipient, overt, vanity, vaunt.*

Tell students to stand if the sentence is true and remain seated if the sentence is false. Read aloud each statement below, and have students stand (or sit) to indicate *true* or *false.*

1.	A braggart is likely to *vaunt* his achievements.	true
2.	A *vanity* is a table for the living room.	false
3.	Light passes onto the lens of a camera through an *aperture*.	true
4.	The *inception* of a process comes at the end.	false
5.	*Overt* anger is obvious and easy to spot.	true
6.	An *incipient* illness is just starting to develop.	true

Lesson 4 Key Word Activity Master (see page 88)

Answers:

1. B

2. A

3. C

4. E

5. D

6. G

7. F

8. H

9–12. Answers will vary.

ASSIGN Exercises

(Book A, pages 24–25)

REVIEW Lessons 3 and 4

Sometimes a limerick can give students a feel for a new word. Display these limericks about a word from Lesson 3 (*pandemonium*) and a word from Lesson 4 (*inception*) and have students orally answer the questions below. (Note that the limericks also use the familiar word *nil* and the key word *preclude* in context.)

Pandemonium	*Inception*
Think "hubbub" and "racket" and "din,"	"The very beginning, the start"
"Uproar from without and within."	Is the meaning I'd like to impart.
It's loud and it's shrill.	I defy any dude
Peace and quiet are nil.	Who would try to *preclude*
Pandemonium makes your head spin.	My defining *inception* by heart.

1. Is *pandemonium* noisy or silent? (noisy)

2. At the *inception* of a process, do you have a finished product? (no)

3. Is a library a place where "peace and quiet are *nil*"? (No, libraries are usually quiet.)

4. If you keep something from happening, have you *precluded* the event? (yes)

Have students write some limericks, couplets, or other rhymes that show the meanings of the words from Lessons 3 and 4. Post a selection of them on your bulletin board.

Possible samples:

I've tried to be social, but what's the use?
I'll stay in my room and become a *recluse*.

When the *trilogy* of songs was played,
An amazing and glorious sound was made.

SELECT Review Exercises

(Book A, page 26)

LESSON 5

Literary and Historical References

8. comply In 1955 Rosa Parks (b. 1923) defied a Montgomery, Alabama, ordinance by refusing to yield her seat in the front of a city bus; her arrest led a local minister, Dr. Martin Luther King, Jr. (1929–1968), to organize a boycott of the bus system.

9. implement Invented by American manufacturer Cyrus Hall McCormick (1809–1884) in 1834, the reaping machine enabled one worker to harvest many acres single-handedly.

Exercise 5B, 2b An advocate of nonviolence, Indian leader Mahatma Gandhi (1869–1948) frequently resorted to personal fasts as a means of influencing political events.

Exercise 5B, 2c Blitzkrieg, or "the Blitz," was a series of intensive air raids launched by Germany against London during World War II for the purpose of demoralizing the populace and weakening English resistance.

INTRODUCE Lesson 5

(Book A, page 27)

Tell students that the theme of Lessons 5 and 6 is "More or Less."

Display, read, and translate the opening quotation from Lesson 5: *Satis eloquentiae, sapientiae parum.* "Enough eloquence, too little wisdom."

- Ask students for restatements in their own words. (possible answer: Skillful speakers may sound great with their *eloquent* delivery, but what they say still might not make sense.)
- Point out that *satis* is a Latin root that means "enough," and it is one of the roots covered in Lesson 5. This ties with the "More or Less" theme by suggesting that sometimes *more eloquence* covers up *less wisdom.*

PREVIEW Familiar Words

(Book A, pages 27–28)

microorganism, microscope, microphone, minus, diminish, minute

ACTIVITY 1: *micro*

Display the familiar words *microorganism, microscope,* and *microphone.* Read them orally, pointing at each one, and then chorally with the class. Underline *micro* in each word.

Ask students the following questions:

- Do you think a *microorganism* is big or small? (Small. Explain that a *microorganism* is so small it cannot be seen with the naked eye.)

- To get a good look at a *microorganism,* what instrument would you use? (A *microscope.* It makes small things look larger.)

- What does a *microphone* do for a small, soft voice? (makes it sound larger, louder)

Ask: What shared meaning for *micro* is in these words? (small)

ACTIVITY 2: *min*

Display the familiar words *minus, diminish,* and *minute.* Read them orally, pointing at each one, and then chorally with the class. Underline *min* in each word.

Ask students the following questions:

- In math, what does *minus* mean? (less, take away from, subtract)
- When you *diminish* something, do you add to it or subtract from it? (subtract)

Tell students that *minute* can be pronounced two ways: mĭ´ nət (1/60 of an hour) or mī nōōt´ (small). A sixty-second *minute* is a small, or *minute,* period of time. Ask your students rhyming riddles, using *minute* (mī nōōt´).

- What is a small apple? (a minute fruit)
- What is a small underground part of a plant? (a minute root)
- What is a small horn? (a minute flute)
- What is a small cowboy shoe? (a minute boot)
- What is a small soft noise made by an owl? (a minute hoot)

Review: The familiar words indicate that both *micro* and *min* suggest meanings connected with "small, tiny, less."

PRESENT Key Words

(Book A, pages 27–30)

Display the Lesson 5 Greek and Latin roots and review their meanings:

- the Greek root *mikros* (*micro*), meaning "small"
- the Latin root *minuo, minuere, minui, minutum,* meaning "to lessen" and *minus,* meaning "less"
- the Latin root *tenuo, tenuare, tenuavi, tenuatum* (*tenu*), meaning "to make thin" and *tenuis* (*tenu*), meaning "thin"
- the Latin root *satis* (*sat*), meaning "enough"
- the Latin roots *impleo, implere, implevi, impletum* (*plen*), meaning "to fill" and *plenus* (*plen*), meaning "full"

Have students read the key words chorally: *attenuate, comply, expletive, implement, microbe, microcosm, minuscule, minutia, replete, satiate, tenuous.*

Present each of the key words by discussing the following:

- pronunciation
- definitions/connections to the root
- sentences
- parts of speech
- word forms

GUIDE Practice

ACTIVITY 1: Where for the Nouns

Display the key words that are nouns so that you can lead a discussion of where they might be found: *implement, minutia, microbe, microcosm, expletive.*

Ask students the following questions:

- Where might you find *implements* for cooking? Building a house? What are those implements? (possible answers: utensils like spoons, spatulas, and whisks are *implements* in a kitchen drawer; tools like hammers and saws are *implements* in a toolbox.)

- Where might you find tiny living organisms called *microbes*? (possible answers: under a microscope in a laboratory, in a doctor's office or a hospital.)

- What is an example of *minutia* in your house? (possible answers: a doll bracelet, a paper clip.)

- Where might you find a *microcosm* of our school? (possible answer: Here in our classroom. This class is a *microcosm* of the whole school.)

- Where might you hear or read an *expletive*? (possible answers: On television, angry people come out with bad words, oaths, and *expletives.* In comic strips you see symbols like "#$%@" for *expletives.*)

ACTIVITY 2: Restatements for the Adjectives and Verbs

Next, display the key words that are adjectives and verbs, with the following one-word definitions of each.

minuscule—tiny   *satiated*—full

tenuous—weak   *attenuate*—lessen

replete—complete   *comply*—obey

Read each sentence containing a key word aloud. Emphasize the italicized key word. Point to the key word as you say it. After each sentence, have your students restate the sentence, using the easy one-word definition of the key word.

1. A crumb is a *minuscule* part of a cake. (restatement: A crumb is a tiny part of a cake.)

2. After Thanksgiving dinner, I was *satiated*. (restatement: After Thanksgiving dinner, I was full.)

3. I saw only a *tenuous* connection between the book and the movie. (restatement: The book and the movie were so different that I saw only a weak connection between them.)

4. The trees *attenuated* the force of the rainstorm. (restatement: The trees lessened the force of the rainstorm.)

5. All students are expected to *comply* with the school rules. (restatement: All students are expected to obey the school rules.)

6. The flower garden was in full bloom, *replete* with ferns. (restatement: The flower garden was in full bloom, complete with ferns.) Point out to students that it's easy to remember that *replete* means *complete* because they both have *plete* on the end. They both come from roots that mean *full*.

To provide more oral practice for students, reverse the preceding activity. You say the restated sentence, and have the students come back with the sentence using the key word.

Lesson 5 Key Word Activity Master (see page 89)

Answers:

1. B
2. C
3. A
4. E
5. D
6. microbe
7. minutia
8. microcosm
9. tenuous
10. minuscule
11. expletive

ASSIGN Exercises

(Book A, pages 30–32)

LESSON 6

Literary and Historical References

1. copious   The more than 1500 letters of Marie de Rabutin Chantal, Marquise de Sévigné (1626–1696), were published posthumously in 1725.

4. magnate   Western Union magnate Ezra Cornell (1807–1874) founded Cornell University in 1865.

Exercise 6B, 2c As he expressed in his Gettysburg Address, Abraham Lincoln (1809–1865) urged a policy of reunification and tolerance between combatants after the Civil War.

Exercise 6B, 4c Alfred Nobel (1833–1896), the inventor of dynamite, provided in his will for annual prizes in the fields of literature, physiology or medicine, chemistry, physics, and the promotion of world peace.

Exercise 6C, 1 In the early twentieth century, William Randolph Hearst (1863–1951) built a powerful chain of American newspapers and magazines.

INTRODUCE Lesson 6

(Book A, page 32)

Remind students that the theme of Lessons 5 and 6 is "More or Less."

Display, read, and translate the opening quotation from Lesson 6: *Magna est veritas et praevalet.* "The truth is great and it will prevail."

- Ask students what the word *prevail* means. (win, overcome, be accepted) What synonyms of *great* would fit in the quotation? (Truth is *powerful, forceful, strong, effective,* and it will prevail.)
- Point out that the first word of the Latin quotation, *magna,* is a form of the Latin root *magnus* which is featured in Lesson 6. This lesson ties with the "More or Less" theme of Lessons 5 and 6 by emphasizing *more* via five different roots. The roots *copia* (plenty), *makros* (large), *magnus* (great), *megas* (great) and *poly* (many) are featured.

PREVIEW Familiar Words

(Book A, pages 32–33)

megaphone, magnify, copy, magnificent

Display the familiar words *megaphone, magnify, copy,* and *magnificent.* Read them orally, pointing at each one, and then chorally with the class.

Ask students the following questions:

- Have a student draw a *megaphone* and a *magnifying glass* on the board. How is each used? (A megaphone can make a person's voice sound louder. A magnifying glass makes a small item look larger.)
- How many *copies* of a paper you would need for the whole class? Explain that it is possible to make just one *copy* at the copying machine. But would you make more than one for the whole class? Would you usually make a few extra *copies,* just in case? (Yes, you usually make lots of copies, a plentiful number, more than enough.) This will lead up to helping students connect the familiar word *copy* and the key word *copious* in this lesson.
- Have the class compile a list of sightseeing attractions that are *magnificent.* (Accept all suggestions of places that are large, great, or impressive, such as the Statue of Liberty, Grand Canyon, even a major roller coaster.) Are any of these magnificent attractions tiny or small? (no)

Review: The familiar words indicate that *mega, magnus,* and *copia* suggest "large, great, plentiful."

PRESENT Key Words

(Book A, pages 32–34)

Display the Lesson 6 Greek and Latin roots and review their meanings:

- the Latin root *copia* meaning "plenty"
- the Greek root *makros* (*macro*), meaning "large"
- the Latin root *magnus,* meaning "great"
- the Greek root *megas,* meaning "great"
- the Greek root *poly,* meaning "many"

Have students read the key words chorally: *copious, macrocosm, magnanimous, magnate, magnitude, megalomania, polygamy, polygon.*

Present each of the key words by discussing the following:

- pronunciation
- definitions/connections to the root
- sentences
- parts of speech
- word forms

GUIDE Practice

True or False

Have students print TRUE on a piece of green paper, and FALSE on a piece of red paper. Tell them to listen to each key word and sentence that you read aloud, decide whether the sentence is true or false, and mentally select the proper paper.

Then, on a signal from you, they should close their eyes and hold up either TRUE (green paper) or FALSE (red paper). This way, you can prevent copycat answering, and you can tell at a glance which students are correct and incorrect.

1. *Copious:* A copious supply of shirts would fill a drawer.   true
2. *Macrocosm:* A macrocosm is smaller than a microcosm.   false
3. *Magnanimous:* A magnanimous person deserves thanks.   true
4. *Magnate:* A magnate earns a very small salary.   false
5. *Magnitude:* The magnitude of our solar system is impressive.   true
6. *Megalomaniac:* A megalomaniac does not think he is very important.   false
7. *Polygon:* A polygon can have six or seven sides.   true
8. *Polygamy:* Polygamy is the practice of having more than one spouse.   true

Stop and have students defend their answers whenever you see a mix of red and green responses. With the help of the dictionary, teams of students can compose additional true or false sentences in which they use the key words.

Lesson 6 Key Word Activity Master (see page 90)

Answers:

1. polygamy
2. polygon
3. megaphone
4. macrocosm
5. magnanimity
6. megalomania
7. *magnitude* and *magnate*
8. *copying* and *copious*
9. *magnate* and *magnanimous*
10. *magnifying* and *magnificent*
11–12. Answers will vary.

ASSIGN Exercises

(Book A, pages 34–36)

REVIEW Lessons 5 and 6

Remind your students that the theme of Lessons 5 and 6 was "More or Less." Display the words below in random order, *not* in the pairs as shown. Have your students race to form these pairs of antonyms that reflect "More or Less": *macrocosm/microcosm, satiate*/starve, *comply*/refuse, *magnanimous*/stingy, strong/*tenuous,* huge/*minuscule, copious*/scarce. Students can work independently or as teams.

You will also want to review the following words: *polygon, implement, expletive, polygamist, megalomaniac, magnate, minutia, microbe, replete, magnitude, attenuate.* Have students divide this list into words they can depict in drawings and words they can't. The words are increasingly difficult to represent pictorially. Some students will attempt only the first two, but others may create scenes that represent even the final words. Students who are not as comfortable with visual representations are encouraged to write descriptive sentences that use the words in context based on other students' pictures.

SELECT Review Exercises

(Book A, page 37)

LESSON 7

Literary and Historical References

1. antebellum   Written by Margaret Mitchell (1900–1949), *Gone With the Wind* was a best-selling novel that was made into a Academy Award-winning film.

2. antecedent   The Germanic language Anglo-Saxon (also called Old English), spoken in England between the eighth and twelfth centuries, is the primary source of modern English.

4. avant-garde   An artistic style originating in late nineteenth-century France, Impressionism sought to capture a visual impression of a particular moment using pure primary colors and bold brushwork.

5. vanguard   The vastly outnumbered English troops of King Henry V (1387–1422) defeated an army of mounted French knights at Agincourt in 1415.

In intentional contrast to the nobility, partisans of the French Revolution eschewed wigs and wore their hair unpowdered.

Exercise 7B, 1b   Following the stock market crash of 1929, a period of radical decline in the national economy known as the Great Depression caused thousands to be unemployed and millions to live in poverty.

Exercise 7B, 2b   In 1588 the English ships of Queen Elizabeth I defeated the "invincible" Armada sent by Spain's King Phillip II to conquer the English navy.

Exercise 7B, 2c   Both the public and private buildings of American architect Frank Lloyd Wright (1869–1959) illustrate his dictum that form should follow function.

Exercise 7B, 3d   Gautama Siddhartha (563?–483 B.C.?), whose title of The Buddha means "the enlightened one," taught the principles that became Buddhism, which include nonviolence to all living things.

Exercise 7B, 5a   In Shakespeare's play *Julius Caesar*, the protagonist defies several warnings, including his wife's dream, and attends the Senate, where an assassination awaits him.

Exercise 7C, 4   Although Polonius in Shakespeare's *Hamlet* is characterized by his long-windedness, his advice to his son Laertes has become famous: "And this above all, to thine own self be true. ..."

Exercise 7C, 7   In Charles Dickens's novel *Little Dorrit* (1857), the impoverished Dorrit family illustrates the horrors of debtors' prisons and the folly of class snobbery.

INTRODUCE Lesson 7

(Book A, page 38)

Tell students that the theme of Lessons 7 and 8 is "Before and After."

Display, read, and translate the opening quotation from Lesson 7: *Praemonitus, praemunitus.* "Forewarned is forearmed."

- Ask students to paraphrase the opening quotation. (possible answer: When you are told in advance what is coming, you can be prepared for it. This saying applies well to tests in school. If you are forewarned on Monday that there will be a quiz on Friday, you can forearm yourself with knowledge all week and do well on the quiz.)
- Point out that the quotation ties with the "Before and After" theme of Lesson 7 by emphasizing the *before* part (*fore*warned, *fore*armed). The Latin root *pre* meaning "before" is featured in the lesson.

PREVIEW Familiar Words

(Book A, page 40)

precaution, precede, predict, prefix, prepare, prevent

Display the familiar words *precaution, precede, predict, prefix, prepare,* and *prevent.* Read them orally, pointing at each one, and then chorally with the class. Underline *pre* in each word.

Ask students the following questions:

- What *precautions* should you take against sunburn? (Apply sunscreen *before* spending time outdoors.) What *precautions* against mosquito bites? (Apply bug repellent **before** going outside.)
- If you *precede* someone in line, do you walk behind that person? (No, you walk **before** that person.)
- Do you *predict* the future or the past? (Future. You predict something **before** it happens.)
- Name some common *prefixes.* (un, re, dis). List words that start with these prefixes. (unhappy, unable, undo; return, renew, rebuild; dissatisfied, disappear, disagree.) Where does the prefix appear? (at the beginning, **before** the rest of the word)
- Do you *prepare* a meal after eating? (no, **before** eating)
- How do you *prevent* catching measles? (You get a vaccination **before** you are exposed to the disease.)

Ask: What meaning do you associate with the prefix *pre?* (before)

PRESENT Key Words

(Book A, pages 38–40)

Display the Lesson 7 Latin roots and review their meanings:

- the Latin root *ante*, meaning "before"
- the Latin root *pre*, meaning "before"

Have students read the key words chorally: *antebellum, antecedent, anterior, avant-garde, precept, predestination, preempt, premonition, preposterous, pretentious, vanguard.*

Present each of the key words by discussing the following:

- pronunciation
- definitions/connections to the root
- sentences
- parts of speech
- word forms

GUIDE Practice

Context Activity

Tell students that the passage you are going to read aloud contains most of the key words from Lesson 7. They should simply listen to your first and second oral readings of the passage to get an idea of the intent and content. During your third reading, pause at the end of each sentence. Ask students to define the underlined word. Context should help students come up with definitions similar to those that appear after the passage.

Passage for oral reading

Obey these <u>precepts</u>:

1. Don't wear <u>antebellum</u> hoopskirts to school.

2. Don't wear <u>avant-garde</u> hats-of-the-future to school.

3. It would be <u>preposterous</u> to wear a swimsuit to school.

4. Don't dress <u>pretentiously</u>, as if you wanted to impress everybody.

Obeying these rules is taking <u>preemptive</u> action to avoid punishment.

You should have a <u>premonition</u> that bad things will happen if you disobey these rules.

But you'll be <u>predestined</u> for success if you obey the preceding precepts.

Probable definitions of underlined words

precepts: rules

antebellum: before a war, specifically before the American Civil War

avant-garde: styles that are ahead of the times

preposterous: so out-of-place as to be funny

pretentiously: in a showy manner

preemptive: ahead of time

premonition: a feeling in advance

predestined: fated, sure to happen

Lesson 7 Key Word Activity Master (see page 91)

Answers:

1. Y
2. Y
3. N
4. Y
5. pretentious
6. premonition
7. antebellum
8. anterior
9. preposterous
10. precept
11. B
12. A
13. D
14. C
15. E

ASSIGN Exercises

(Book A, pages 41–43)

LESSON 8

Literary and Historical References

1. premier
Russian-born Golda Meir (1898–1978) emigrated first to the United States and then to Israel, where she served as prime minister from 1969–1974.

2. primate
After English King Henry VIII (1491–1547) denied the authority of the Pope in England, he appointed the Archbishop of Canterbury head of the newly established protestant Church of England.

8. posthumous
The journal kept by Anne Frank (1929–1945), a German Jewish teenager, during her family's years of hiding from Nazi internment has become a classic of Holocaust literature.

Exercise 8B, 1a
Charles Darwin (1809–1882) set forth his theory of evolution by natural selection in *On the Origin of Species* (1859).

Exercise 8B, 1c
American baseball player George Herman Ruth (1895–1948), who was known as "the Bambino" or "Babe," held the American League batting record for many years.

Exercise 8B, 2a
As a carrier of hemophilia, a genetic disease conveyed through the maternal line, Queen Victoria passed the disease on to many members of the royal family.

Exercise 8B, 3b
English poet Gerard Manley Hopkins (1844–1889) stopped writing and burned his youthful poetry when he was ordained a Jesuit priest. He returned to writing in the last years of his life, but these works were published only after his death by his friend, the poet laureate Robert Bridges.

Exercise 8B, 5a
American poet Henry Wadsworth Longfellow (1807–1882) is best known for his narrative poems on historical subjects, such as *Evangeline, Hiawatha,* and *The Courtship of Miles Standish.*

Exercise 8C, 3
American author Edgar Allan Poe (1809–1849) wrote both famous poetry such as "The Raven" and suspenseful short stories such as "The Tell-Tale Heart" and "The Cask of Amontillado" as well as literary criticism.

INTRODUCE Lesson 8

(Book A, page 43)

Remind students that the theme of Lessons 7 and 8 is "Before and After."

Display, read, and translate the opening quotation from Lesson 8: *Primus inter pares*. "The first among equals."

- Explain to students that the expression, "The first among equals," is used in many governing bodies. Consider the student council. The president of the student council is the leader, so in that sense she is *first*. In what sense is she *equal*? (Like all the other members, she has just one vote.)
- Point out that the first word of the Latin quotation is *primus. Primus* is also one of the Latin roots featured in Lesson 8. It ties with the "Before and After" theme of Lessons 7 and 8 by emphasizing the *before* part, "first."

PREVIEW Familiar Words

(Book A, pages 43–44)

primary, primer, primitive, postgraduate, postscript, postwar

ACTIVITY 1: *primus*

Display the familiar words *primary, primer,* and *primitive*. Read them orally, pointing at each one, and then chorally with the class. Underline *pri* in each word.

Ask students the following questions:

- What grades are the *primary* grades in school? (kindergarten to third grade, the grades that came **first**)
- In what grades did you read a book called a *primer*? (kindergarten and/or **first** grade)
- Is the president of the United States's house a *primitive* dwelling? (No, it is not like the **first** kinds of houses ever built. It is modern.)

Ask: What shared meaning for *pri* is in these words? (First.)

ACTIVITY 2: *post*

Display the familiar words *postgraduate, postscript,* and *postwar.* Read them orally, pointing at each one, and then chorally with the class. Underline *post* in each word.

Ask students the following questions:

- Suppose you write a letter, finish it, sign it, and them think of something else that you want to add. You can put a "PS" at the end of the letter. Look at the words on the board. Which one do you think PS stands for? (*postscript,* which means "written after")
- Suppose a college graduate takes a class she had no time for when she was an still in school. Which of the words on display might describe that course? (*postgraduate*)
- Suppose a soldier writes a book after he retires from military service. What might be the title of that book? (possible answers: *My Postwar Experiences* or *After the Fighting: My Postwar Opinions.*)

Ask: What shared meaning for *post* is in these words? (after)

Review: The familiar words indicate that *pri* can suggest "first, beginning, before," and *post* can suggest "after."

PRESENT Key Words

(Book A, pages 43–45)

Display the Lesson 8 Latin roots and review their meanings:

- the Latin root *primus (pri),* meaning "first"
- the Latin root *post,* meaning "after"

Have students read the key words chorally: *premier, primate, prime, primeval, primordial, posterior, posterity, posthumous.*

Present each of the key words by discussing the following:

- pronunciation
- definitions/connections to the root
- sentences
- parts of speech
- word forms

The *Nota Bene* on page 45 points out the *ante* and *post* connections with A.M. and P.M.

GUIDE Practice

ACTIVITY 1: True or False

Have students print TRUE on a piece of green paper, and FALSE on a piece of red paper. Tell them to listen to each key word and sentence that you read aloud, decide whether the sentence is true or false, and mentally select the proper paper.

Then, on a signal from you, they should close their eyes and hold up either TRUE (green paper) or FALSE (red paper). This way, you can prevent copycat answering, and you can tell at a glance which students are correct and incorrect.

1. *Premier:* The *premier* brands of athletic shoes are the least expensive.   false

2. *Primate:* Some *primates* can use sign language to communicate.   true

3. *Prime:* A *prime* location for a picnic is one with some shade, some sun, a table, and no ants.   true

4. *Primeval:* The groves of *primeval* trees were planted recently.   false

5. *Primordial:* Dinosaurs lived in *primordial* times.   true

6. *Posterior:* The *posterior* section is in the front.   false

7. *Posterity:* Your grandparents are your *posterity.*   false

8. *Posthumous:* When a letter arrives *posthumously,* its writer is already dead.   true

Stop and have students defend their answers whenever you see a mix of red and green responses. With the help of the dictionary, teams of students can compose more true-false sentences in which they use the key words.

Lesson 8 Key Word Activity Master (see page 92)

Answers:

1. posthumous

2. posterior

3. *primeval* and *primordial*

4. *premier* and *prime*

5. D

6. C

7. A

8. B

9–12. Answers will vary.

ASSIGN Exercises

(Book A, pages 45–47)

REVIEW Lessons 7 and 8

Frequency

Ask students:

- Of the nineteen key words in Lessons 7 and 8 (with the "Before and After" theme), how many are "After" words? (only three) What characteristic do the three words share? (They all begin with *post.*)

- How many key words are "Before" words? (sixteen)

- In the gray boxes in Lessons 7 and 8, where Familiar Words are listed, how many "After" words do you find? (three) What characteristic do they share? (All of them begin with *post.*)

- You learned three "Before" prefixes: *ante, pre,* and *pri.* How many familiar words begin with each of the "Before" prefixes? (Two familiar words begin with *ante.* Fourteen familiar words begin with *pre.* Seven familiar words begin with *pri.*)

Have students use a dictionary to see if the frequencies in their book are paralleled in the dictionary listings. Remind them that not every word that starts with *ante, pre, pri,* and *post* carries a "Before or After" meaning, but quite a few do. (Examples of exceptions: *antelope, pressure, pride, posture.*) Write *ante, pre, pri,* and *post* on the board. Under each prefix, make a list of words from the dictionary that carry the "Before" or "After" meaning.

SELECT Review Exercises

(Book A, page 48)

LESSON 9

Literary and Historical References

2. artifice
The Greek storyteller Aesop (620–560 B.C.) is credited as the author of Aesop's Fables. His sources were, however, probably earlier literature.

3. artless
Daughter of Prospero in *The Tempest* by Shakespeare (1564–1616), Miranda has never before seen a man other than her father and quickly falls in love with young Ferdinand, who has been shipwrecked on her island.

4. artisan
English craftsperson George Hepplewhite (d. 1786) designed and constructed cabinets, chairs, firescreens, and tables—the tables were often inlaid with woods of various colors.

5. ode
For poets of the Romantic period, among them Percy Bysshe Shelley (1792–1822), the ode was a familiar form allowing expression of personal feelings about nature.

6. parody
American writer Ogden Nash (1902–1971) is noted for his humorous verse, often marked by uneven line length and playful rhyme.

8. incantation
In the story "Ali Baba and the Forty Thieves" the incantation, "Open, Sesame," causes a rock in front of a cave to open like a door. Through this door comes a band of robbers carrying bags of gold. By overhearing this password, Ali Baba manages to acquire a fortune but cannot enjoy it until he has rid himself of the forty thieves. The story, one of Scheherazade's *Arabian Nights'* entertainments, so diverts the king that he does not indulge in his chronic habit of killing each new wife the day after the marriage. These Arabian, Indian, and Persian stories appeared between the eighth and sixteenth centuries; they began to be collected in the thirteenth century.

9. recant
Faced with pressure to conform to church belief in a geocentric rather than heliocentric universe, Galileo (1564–1642) recanted what he knew to be true.

10. depict

A colorfully embroidered strip of linen eighty yards long and nineteen inches wide, the medieval Bayeux Tapestry depicts events preceding and during the Norman Conquest of England (1066) when William the Conqueror defeated Harold the Saxon.

Jade Snow Wong (b. 1922) has said that she wrote *Fifth Chinese Daughter* (1950) in an attempt to create understanding between Chinese and Americans at a time when little had been written about the collision of cultures in the lives of young Chinese immigrants.

11. pictograph

Lasting for 2,000 years in Mexico and Central America, the Mayan civilization produced pyramids, a reliable calendar, and astrological observations as well as art forms preserved on stone monuments.

Exercise 9B, 1b

The Greek goddess Artemis, the twin sister of Apollo, is the moon goddess pledged to chastity, huntress and guardian of wild beasts, patroness of youth, and lover of music and dancing.

Exercise 9B, 1d

In Shakespeare's play *Macbeth* the three witches reveal to the title character the dramatic rise to power in store for him. This news stimulates him to hasten his acquisition of that power by taking the lives of those who appear to stand in his way: King Duncan, friend Banquo, and others.

Exercise 9B, 2d

Although Joan of Arc (1412?–1431), French saint and heroine, had led the forces of the Dauphin Charles VII to victory, she was judged to have violated religious principles with her visions and was burned at the stake.

Exercise 9B, 3a

Frankie Addams is the creation of American novelist Carson McCullers (1917–1967) in *The Member of the Wedding*. An adaptation of this novel won a Critic's Award in 1950 as the best play of the year.

Exercise 9B, 4a

Using the pseudonym Carolyn Keene, Harriet Stratemeyer Adams (1883–1982) created mysteries for Nancy Drew to solve in forty-seven novels from *Secret of the Old Clock* in 1930 to *Invisible Intruder* in 1969. Continuing to use pseudonyms, Adams wrote other series familiar to many young people: Dana Girls, Hardy Boys, Bobbsey Twins, and Tom Swift Jr.

Exercise 9B, 4b	As described in Homer's ninth-century B.C. epic poem *The Odyssey*, Penelope successfully keeps her suitors at bay during her husband Odysseus's twenty-year absence.
Exercise 9B, 4c	Disguised as a man, Deborah Sampson (1760–1827) became a soldier in the Revolutionary War. Her identity was discovered, but she enlisted again, trained at West Point, and fought in combat, remaining unrecognized until she was hospitalized. Needing money to support her family in later years, she lectured about her war experiences to eager audiences.
Exercise 9C, 1	The Toltec civilization, which preceded the Aztec, practiced sun worship and human sacrifice. Its achievements included the building of pyramids, the smelting of metals, and the development of a calendar cycle.
Exercise 9C, 2	American artist Mary Cassatt (1845–1926) is best known for her paintings of women and children in a style influenced by the Impressionists.
Exercise 9C, 3	Ernest L. Thayer (1863–1940) tells Casey's story in thirteen four-line stanzas. Despite Casey's optimism, easy manner, proud bearing, and genial response to cheers ("he lightly doffed his hat" standing at the plate), the Mudville nine are out of luck (stanza thirteen) because "mighty Casey has struck out."
Exercise 9C, 6	Only the wily Moriarity poses real problems for Sherlock Holmes, the detective invented by Sir Arthur Conan Doyle (1859–1930).

INTRODUCE Lesson 9

(Book A, page 51)

Tell students that the theme of Lessons 9 and 10 is "Creativity."

Display, read, and translate the opening quotation from Lesson 9: *Ars longa, vita brevis.* "Art is long; life is short."

- Ask students to describe a painting that was done before they were born. (possible answers: portrait of an ancestor or a famous person from history, battle scene or pastoral scene from times past) Do some pieces of art last longer than a person's lifetime? (yes)
- Point out that *ars* (the first word in the Latin quotation) is a Latin root that means "art," and is one of the roots covered in Lesson 9. It ties with the "Creativity " theme.

PREVIEW Familiar Words

(Book A, pages 52–55)

art, artist, artistry, picture, pictorial, picturesque

ACTIVITY 1: *ars, artis*

Display the familiar words *art, artist* and *artistry*. Read them orally, pointing at each one, and then chorally with the class. Underline *art* in each word.

Ask students the following questions:

- What do you think of when you hear the word *art*? (Drawing and painting will probably be the first responses from students. Help them extend their thinking to include singing, dancing, even language *arts*.)
- Is a creative and skillful photographer an *artist*? (yes) A sculptor? (yes)
- Can writers show *artistry* in their choice of words? (Yes. A writer can use words to create a picture in your mind's eye.)

Ask: What is the shared meaning for *art* in these words? (all the creative arts)

ACTIVITY 2: *pingo, pictum*

Display the familiar words *picture, pictorial,* and *picturesque*. Read them orally, pointing at each one, and then chorally with the class. Underline *pict* in each word.

Ask students the following questions:

- Where do you see *pictures*? (possible answers: in the classroom, art museum, newspapers, magazines, books, online, everywhere)
- You have seen *pictorial* representations outdoors. Where? (possible answers: children on school crossing signs, tents on camping area signs, road signs to show curves and construction) How about *pictorial* representations indoors? Where? (possible answers: decorations on paper plates, embroidery)
- Some works of art are *picturesque* and some are not. Is a landscape painting of tornado damage *picturesque*? (no) An operating room at a hospital? (no) A flower garden in a pretty park? (yes) A picnic scene on a hillside in sunny weather? (yes) A scene of a cottage surrounded by greenery, embroidered with bright threads on cloth? (yes)

Ask: What is the shared meaning for *pict* in these words? (the form of art represented in pictures)

Review: The familiar words indicate that ars suggests "all the creative arts," and that *pict* suggests "the forms of art represented in pictures (e.g., paintings and embroidery.)

PRESENT Key Words

(Book A, pages 52–55)

Display the Lesson 9 Greek and Latin roots and review their meanings:

- the Latin root *ars, artis* (*art*), meaning "art "
- the Greek root *aoide* (*ode*), meaning "song"
- the Latin root *canto, cantare, cantavi, cantatum* (*cant*), meaning "to sing"
- the Latin root *pingo, pingere, pinxi, pictum* (*pict*), meaning "to paint, to embroider"

Have students read the key words on page 51 chorally: *artifact, artifice, artisan, artless, depict, incantation, ode, parody, pictograph, recant, rhapsody.*

Present each of the key words by discussing the following:

- pronunciation
- definitions/connections to the root
- sentences
- parts of speech
- word forms

The *Nota Benes* on pages 53 and 54 present interesting material on odes, parodies, and rhapsodies.

GUIDE Practice

Sorting

Display the key words in random order (not alphabetical). Have students sort the words into the following meaning groups: *art, pict, cant,* and *od.* This sorting activity should result in these four groups of words:

art: *artifact, artifice, artisan, artless*

pict: *depict, pictograph*

cant: *incantation, recant*

od: *ode, parody, rhapsody*

Divide the class into four groups. Have each group teach two of its words to the class.

Sort the key words again, this time, based on part of speech: adjective, verb, or noun. This sorting will result in these groups:

adjective: *artless*

verbs: *depict, recant*

nouns: *artisan, artifact, artifice, pictograph, incantation, ode, parody, rhapsody.*

- Which noun is a person, skilled in a craft? (artisan)
- Which noun is a chant? (incantation)
- Which is meant to be funny? (parody)
- Which is most likely to break if you drop it? (artifact)
- Which would a serious poet like to write? (ode)
- Which is most likely to have been drawn on the wall of a cave? (pictograph)
- Which can be a form of trickery? (artifice)
- Which can refer to music? (rhapsody)

Lesson 9 Key Word Activity Master (see page 93)

Answers:

1. *artisan* and *artifice*
2. *depicted* and *pictographs*
3. *recanted* and *incantations*
4. *rhapsody* and *ode*
5. *artless* and *artifacts*
6. E
7. D
8. C
9. B
10. A

ASSIGN Exercises

(Book A, pages 55–57)

LESSON 10

Literary and Historical References

4. beneficence

By executive order of President John F. Kennedy, the Peace Corps came into being on March 1, 1961. At the request of governments around the world, it sends American citizens to assist with projects such as water supply and construction of dams in programs of health, agriculture, education, and community development.

5. efficacious

Samuel Johnson (1709–1784), English poet, essayist, and critic, became known for pithy statements in both conversation and writing. He was also the composer of the *Dictionary of the English Language* (1755), the first work offering definitions and examples of English words in use.

8. faction

English author William Golding (b. 1911–1993) depicts the struggles for dominance between two groups of marooned boys who vie for power as they wrangle over ways to survive.

10. mollify

The fable about the unmollified peacock is credited to Aesop.

11. context

The reason for hope to listeners of the Fifth Symphony was that in the first two measures of the first movement the sequence of notes (three eighth notes followed by a dotted half note) represents in Morse Code the letter *v* (dot-dot-dot-dash), the symbol for victory. German musician Ludwig von Beethoven (1770–1827) composed nine symphonies as well as concertos, sonatas, and other works.

Exercise 10B, 1a

John Philip Sousa (1854–1932), American composer and band master, became known as the "March King" for his military marches and band arrangements. One of his most familiar marches is "Stars and Stripes Forever."

Exercise 10B, 2d

American Lydia Pinkham (1819–1883) is best known as the inventor of a remedy for many physical complaints; it was a concoction of medicinal roots, seeds, and 18 percent alcohol.

Exercise 10B, 4c

Using the pseudonym Lewis Carroll, Charles Lutwidge Dodgson (1832–1898), English clergyman, parodied the style of heroic poetry in *The Hunting of the Snark*. The story tells of the search for the snark, an imaginary animal named Boojam, who is both elusive and dangerous. Carroll also entertained the children of friends with *Alice's Adventures in Wonderland*.

Exercise 10B, 4d

American artist Georgia O'Keeffe (1887–1986) has achieved recognition by the public as well as by art connoisseurs. Her paintings of flowers and of landscapes of the southwestern United States appear often in reproductions on posters and calendars.

Exercise 10B, 5d   When Maya Lin, a Yale University student of architecture, first won approval for her design of the Vietnam War Memorial to be constructed on the Mall in Washington, D.C., objections were numerous. Opponents disliked the wide V shape, the black granite of the wall, and the absence of the Memorial military figures and inscriptions. However, since the dedication of the Memorial on November 19, 1982, public response has been overwhelmingly favorable toward the simplicity of the design and the long wall containing more than 58,000 names of dead and missing American men and women who served in Vietnam.

Exercise 10B, 8c   Homer (9th century B.C.) tells the story of the Trojan War in the epic poem *The Iliad*. After ten years of on-and-off warfare, the Greeks finally have the upper hand when the Trojans accept as a gift a huge wooden horse. Within its belly are Odysseus (Ulysses) and other Greek heroes who at night attack and conquer the city of Troy.

Exercise 10B, 8d   Without officially declaring war, Germany invaded Poland, Denmark, Norway, Belgium, the Netherlands, Luxembourg, and France in 1939 and 1940.

INTRODUCE Lesson 10

(Book A, page 58)

Remind students that the theme of Lessons 9 and 10 is "Creativity."

Display, read, and translate the opening quotation from Lesson 10: *Facile princeps.* "Easily the leader."

- Ask students if they know the English word *facile*. It is one of the key words in Lesson 10. Have them read the definition on page 59. How does the definition connect with the translation? (*Facile* is defined as "preceeding with ease." The translation of the Latin quotation starts with the word *easily*.)
- Point out that the Latin word *facile* is the first word of the quotation. The Latin root *facio* meaning "to make" is one of the roots covered in Lesson 10. It ties with the "Creativity" theme, since creating often involves making.

PREVIEW Familiar Words

(Book A, pages 59–60)

faculty, affect, textile, textbook, texture

ACTIVITY 1: *facio*

Display the familiar words *faculty* and *affect*. Read them orally, pointing at each one, and then chorally with the class. Underline *fac* in *faculty* and *fec* in *affect*.

Ask students the following questions:

- Who are the *faculty* of our school? (the teachers) What do faculty members do? (They make or develop the curriculum through which students learn.)
- How do motivated students *affect* the faculty? (Motivated students make them happy.)

Ask: What is the shared meaning of *fac* and *fec* in these words? (making)

ACTIVITY 2: *texo*

Display the familiar words *textile, textbook,* and *texture*. Read them orally, pointing at each one, and then chorally with the class. Underline *text* in each word.

Ask students the following questions:

- Which familiar word is a synonym of *cloth*? (*textile*)
- Which familiar word refers to the feel of the cloth? (*texture*)
- Point out that weaving of textiles used to be done by hand on looms. Textiles are now woven in factories. Ask if anyone knows the connection between textiles and *textbooks*. (Cloth covers. You may need to explain that all books used to have cloth covers; this practice is uncommon now.)

Ask: What is the shared meaning for *text* in these words? (weaving)

Review: The familiar words indicate that *fac* and *fec* suggest "making," and *text* suggests "weaving."

PRESENT Key Words

(Book A, pages 58–60)

Display the Lesson 10 Latin roots and review their meanings:

- the Latin root *cresco, crescere, crevi, cretum* (*cre*), meaning "to grow, to increase"
- the Latin root *facio, facere, feci, factum* (*fec, fic, fac*), meaning "to make"
- the Latin root *texo, texeri, texui, textum* (*text*), meaning "to weave"

Have students read the key words on page 58 chorally: *accrue, beneficence, context, crescendo, efficacious, excrescence, facile, facsimile, faction, mollify, pretext.*

Present each of the key words by discussing the following:

- pronunciation
- definitions/connections to the root
- sentences
- parts of speech
- word forms

The *Nota Benes* on pages 58 and 60 extend the derivations from the roots, and point out connections among roots. *Texo* ("to weave"), for example, is closely connected to the Latin root *tego* ("to cover") and the Greek root *tekna* ("art, craft").

GUIDE Practice

Would you enjoy … ?

The key words for this lesson fit well into "Would you enjoy … ?" questions. The answer for each question should promote a "why or why not" discussion among the students.

Ask each question orally, emphasizing the key word. Encourage complete answers with explanations from students (not just *yes* or *no*). Have students look back at the definitions in their books, if necessary.

1. Would you enjoy *beneficence* from your friend? (Yes, because beneficence is kindness and good will.)

2. Would you enjoy a *pretext* of beneficence from your friend? (No, because my friend would be faking. A pretext is not real and genuine.)

3. Would you enjoy being unable to *mollify* a crying infant? (No, because the baby would keep on crying, despite all efforts. It would not calm down.)

4. Would you enjoy finding an *efficacious* way to mollify the infant? (Yes, because an efficacious way would work. It would make the baby stop crying.)

5. Would you enjoy an ongoing *crescendo* of your favorite song? (No, because it would keep on getting louder and louder until it was deafening.)

6. Would you enjoy *accruing* interest on money you had saved? (Yes, because the money would grow and increase. The interest would be added to the savings.)

7. Would you enjoy figuring out the meaning of a word from *context*? (Yes, because figuring out words from context helps me increase my vocabulary and understand what I read better.)

8. Would you enjoy reading a *facsimile* of the original manuscript of *Robinson Crusoe*? (Probably not, since an exact copy would be in handwriting rather than print, and therefore hard to decipher. Daniel Defoe wrote *Robinson Crusoe* over two hundred years ago.)

9. Would you enjoy *facilitating* the flow of traffic in lunch lines? (Yes, because a good facilitator would make it easier to get food quickly.)

10. Would you enjoy belonging to a *faction* who favored shorter lunch periods? (No, because the people in that faction would be an unpopular group since most students want longer lunch periods.)

11. Would you enjoy decorating your room with mythical creatures covered in *excrescences*? (Probably not, because the extra limbs and growths often make those creatures look scary.)

Point out this poetic connection between the key word *pretext* and its *text* root, meaning "to weave."

> What a tangled web we weave
> When first we practice to deceive.

A *pretext* (a false reason put forth to conceal a true one) is the "tangled web we *weave*."

Lesson 10 Key Word Activity Master (see page 94)

Answers:

1. C
2. D
3. E
4. A
5. B
6. facilitate
7. mollify
8. crescendo
9. facsimile
10. B
11. D
12. A
13. E
14. C

ASSIGN Exercises

(Book A, pages 61–63)

REVIEW Lessons 9 and 10

The theme of these lessons is "Creativity," and many of the key words are connected with areas of artistic creativity. Have students look back at the key words on pages 51–60 and group the ones that fit under the headings below. Some words can fit under more than one heading.

Area of Art	Possible Answers
poetry	ode, parody, rhapsody
music	crescendo, incantation, rhapsody
crafts	artisan, artifact, excrescence
drawing	depict, pictograph

To help students examine the key words from another point of view, have them group the words that fit under each of these headings:

Positive Words	Negative Words	Words That Can Be Positive or Negative
beneficence	recant	artifice (skill or trickery)
efficacious	excrescence	facile (easy or superficial)
rhapsodize	pretext	artless (natural or ignorant)
accrue		faction (subgroup or conflict)
mollify		

SELECT Review Exercises

(Book A, pages 63–64)

LESSON 11

Literary and Historical References

1. transgress
In the first book of the Bible, Genesis, the serpent tempts Eve to eat the fruit of the tree of knowledge by saying, "For God doth know that in the day ye eat thereof, then your eyes shall be opened, and ye shall be as gods, knowing good and evil." When Adam joins Eve in violating God's command, both learn that they are banished forever from the Garden of Eden.

5. ambience
Although pollution has eroded the surfaces of statues and buildings, and the city itself is sinking—high tides seasonally flood St. Mark's Square—the city of Venice remains a lure to tourists and a historical and artistic landmark in Italy.

6. obituary
As a mother of nine children, Harriet Beecher Stowe (1811–1896) acquired experience which made her particularly sensitive to difficulties facing African American slave women: unceasing work and the sorrows of separation from their children. *Uncle Tom's Cabin: or, Life among the Lowly* (1852) expresses Stowe's sympathy for the abolitionist cause.

9. erratic
In writing *Alice's Adventures in Wonderland* (1865) and *Through the Looking-Glass* (1872), Charles Lutwidge Dodgson (1832–1898), using the pseudonym Lewis Carroll, expresses something of the strangeness that many children feel in the process of growing up.

10. episode
Both a serious and a popular writer, Frances Hodgson Burnett (1849–1924) published *The Secret Garden* in 1911. Central character Mary Lennox discovers a secret garden, makes friends with a boy named Dickon, and helps another boy recover from his illness through the beneficent effects of the garden.

11. exodus
During the years of the Spanish Civil War (1936–1939) fighting among diverse factions forced many people to leave the country. The war began when the Second Spanish Republic was overthrown by conservative forces. In 1939 General Francisco Franco led his Nationalists to power in Spain.

According to the Book of Exodus, God designates Moses to lead his people out of slavery in Egypt to the promised land Canaan. Although reluctant, Moses is successful, with God's help, in counteracting the difficulties his people and the Egyptian pharaoh place in his way.

Exercise 11B, 1c	The company founded in New York by Louis Comfort Tiffany (1848–1933) developed methods and styles of glassmaking, producing stained glass windows and mosaics and introducing iridescent glass lamp shades and vases. An artist and patron of the arts, Tiffany also designed furniture and room decoration integrating patterns worked in stained glass.
Exercise 11B, 3a	Through rabbits' eyes, readers of *Watership Down* (1972) by Richard Adams (b. 1920) see human beings as unsympathetic aliens and a colony of rabbits as creatures possessing qualities familiar in human behavior—courage and cowardice, strength and weakness.
Exercise 11B, 3b	The presence of a group of African American writers and artists in the New York City district of Harlem between 1919 and 1939 gave rise to what is now called the Harlem Renaissance.
Exercise 11C, 1	Mary Todd Lincoln (1818–1882) had a very difficult life. She was troubled by psychological problems early in her marriage to Abraham Lincoln, and she suffered intensely following the death of their son Willie in 1862, the assassination of President Lincoln in 1865, and the death of her youngest son Tad in 1871.
Exercise 11C, 5	Although during World War II Japan's Emperor Hirohito seemed an inimical figure to Americans, he was an influential proponent of unconditional surrender following the American bombing of two Japanese cities in 1945. Pressed by the Allies, he disavowed emperial divinity and became, according to the 1946 constitution, "a symbol of the state and of the unity of the people."
Exercise 11C, 6	Louisiana west of the Mississippi River belonged to Spain from 1769 to 1800.

INTRODUCE Lesson 11

(Book A, page 65)

Tell students that the theme of Lessons 11 and 12 is "Travel."

Display, read, and translate the opening quotation from Lesson 11: *Sic transit gloria mundi.* "Thus passes away the glory of this world."

- Ask students to give an example that demonstrates the truth of the opening quotation. (possible answers: Pyramids crumble. We tend to quickly forget heores of yesteryear. Entertainers and athletes have short spans of glory.)
- Point out that *trans* is a Latin root that means "across," and it is one of the roots covered in Lesson 11. It ties with the "Travel" theme.

PREVIEW Familiar Words

(Book A, pages 66–67)

transatlantic, transplant, err, error, erroneous

ACTIVITY 1: *trans*

Display the familiar words *transatlantic* and *transplant*. Read them orally, pointing at each one, and then chorally with the class. Underline *trans* in each word.

Ask students the following questions:

- What is the route, or travel path, of a *transatlantic* flight? (across the Atlantic Ocean)
- What is the route, or travel path, of a *transplanted* bush? (from one location to another, across the yard)

Ask: What is the shared meaning for *trans* in these words? (across)

ACTIVITY 2: *erro*

Display the familiar words, *err, error,* and *erroneous*. Read them orally, pointing at each one, and then chorally with the class. Underline *err* in each word.

Ask students the following questions:

- When you make an *error,* do you wander, or stray, from the correct answer? (yes)
- You may have heard the old saying, "To *err* is human; to forgive, divine." Does everyone *err*—stray or wander away from correct behavior— in some way? (yes) Give examples of how you *err.* (possible answers: forget homework, talk back to parents, make a mistake in any regard)
- If all your test answers were *erroneous,* what would your grade be? (zero)

Ask: What shared meaning for *err* is in the words? (to wander or stray away from what is right or correct)

Review: The familiar words indicate that *trans* suggests "across," and *err* suggests "straying away from what is correct or accepted."

PRESENT Key Words

(Book A, pages 65–68)

Display the Lesson 11 Greek and Latin roots and review their meanings:

- the Latin root *trans,* meaning "across"
- the Latin root *eo, ire, ivi, itum,* meaning "to go"
- the Latin root *erro, errare, erravi, erratum* (*err*), meaning "to wander, to stray"
- the Greek root *hodos* (*od*), meaning "journey"

Have students read the key words on page 65 chorally: *aberration, ambience, episode, erratic, exodus, obituary, transgress, transient, transitive, transitory, translucent.*

Present each of the key words by discussing the following:

- pronunciation
- definitions/connections to the root
- sentences
- parts of speech
- word forms

GUIDE Practice

ACTIVITY 1: What's Wrong?

As you read each sentence aloud, emphasize the key word. Then ask students what is wrong in the sentence. Have them explain why the sentence just could not be.

1. The car had a *translucent* windshield. (That's an accident waiting to happen! The driver could not see through that windshield.)

2. During her recovery, she read her *obituary* in the newspaper. (She did not die; she is recovering. Obituaries are printed only after death.)

3. The word "slept" is a *transitive* verb. (No, a transitive verb has an object. "Slept" is an intransitive verb. It does not have an object.)

4. Convicted criminals have committed no *transgressions.* (They have been found guilty of a crime; they broke the law.)

5. Rules about attending school are *transitory.* (No, those rules are permanent. You must keep attending school.)

6. The student was pleased with his *erratic* grades in math. (He would not be pleased. Most students like to get consistent good grades.)

ACTIVITY 2: Discussion Questions

Display the key words that were not discussed during the "What's Wrong?" activity: *aberrant, ambience, episode, exodus, transient.*

Ask students these questions to promote discussion of these words:

- Which two words are most closely connected with "moving out"? (*Transient* and *exodus.* A *transient* might be just one person who stayed a while and then moved out. An *exodus* is a large-scale move-out of a whole group of people.)
- Describe an *aberrant episode* in the life of George Washington. (Possible answer: He chopped down his father's cherry tree. This was an unusual event, out of character.)
- Which word refers to the pleasant atmosphere or environment of a special place? (*Ambience.*) What place has the kind of *ambience* that you appreciate? (Possible answers: my room, the mall, a bookstore.) Point out that this word is almost always associated with a place.

Lesson 11 Key Word Activity Master (see page 95)

Answers:

1. D
2. C
3. A
4. E
5. B
6. *erratic* and *aberrant*
7. *transgression* and *transitive*
8. *episodes* and *exodus*
9. *obituary* and *ambience*
10. *transient* and *transitory*
11. exodus
12. aberration
13. transients
14. episode
15. ambience

ASSIGN Exercises

(Book A, pages 68–69)

LESSON 12

Literary and Historical References

1. itinerant   American pioneer John Chapman (1774–1845) became known as Johnny Appleseed because for forty years he traveled about in Ohio, Indiana, and Illinois distributing seeds and saplings.

2. itinerary   Sacagawea (1784?–1884?), a member of the Oshone tribe, became a part of the Lewis and Clark exploring expedition from 1804 to 1806. Serving as a guide and translator, she also helped the company avoid catastrophe when they met some of her people on the journey.

One of the two highest peaks in the world, Annapurna, in the Himalaya mountain range, demands utmost care in preparation for a climb.

4. circumvent   The heroine of Shakespeare's play *Twelfth Night,* Viola conceals her identity for protection, having reached a strange shore after a shipwreck. Dressed as a boy, she finds employment in the house of a duke, becomes the object of admiration of a gentlewoman, Olivia, and discovers the twin brother she has given up for lost. All is well by the end of the play: Viola is herself and is loved by Duke Orsino.

6. intervene   Mary Poppins' creator, Australian-born Pamela L. Travers (b. 1906), equips this character with magical powers and an umbrella whose handle is shaped like the head of a parrot.

The map of an island where treasure may be buried interests several characters in *Treasure Island* by Robert Louis Stevenson (1850–1894). Jim thwarts the miscreants who want the treasure as much as he, and through his daring he makes possible its return to the rightful owner.

9. devious   *Walkabout* (1961) by Australian writer James Vance Marshall (1887–1964) contrasts the survival resources of an Aboriginal youth undergoing his ritual walkabout and a stranded town-bred girl and boy whom he aids at a cost to himself.

Although the detectives Miss Marple and Hercule Poirot, created by Dame Agatha Christie (1891–1976), are different in temperament and way of life, they are equally quick in recognizing clues where mystery is concerned. Miss Marple is an elderly woman who lives in a small English village, and M. Poirot is a dapper, middle-aged Belgian and professional sleuth.

10. impervious   Considered the founder of modern nursing, Florence Nightingale (1820–1910) resisted her family's pressure to stay in her native England and instead set out for the Crimea to serve British troops as a nurse. Facing inadequate supplies and horrendous conditions, she vowed to make changes in nursing procedures and became famous for improvements in nursing care.

Exercise 12B, 2b   Throughout *The Odyssey* by the Greek poet Homer (9th century B.C.), the goddess Athena serves Odysseus, giving him encouragement, creating disguises for him, and assisting his wife and son. With her help he returns to Ithaca after a twenty-year absence.

Exercise 12B, 2c   Dorothea Lange (1895–1965), American photographer, achieved prominence for her photographs of midwestern itinerants driven by dust storms to California in search of work. Ansel Adams (1902–1984), also American, experimented with light in his photographs, some of which include one of his favorite subjects, rock formations in Yosemite National Park in California.

Exercise 12B, 3d   Writing for both young people and adults, Madeleine L'Engle (b. 1918) has charmed her younger readers with *A Wrinkle in Time* (1962), *Journey with Jonah* (1967), and *A Ring of Endless Light* (1980), the last about young characters encountering the fifth dimension on their journey into space.

Exercise 12B, 5c   The first woman to cross the Atlantic in an airplane, Amelia Earhart (1897–1937?) earned subsequent world renown as the first woman to fly the same route solo.

Exercise 12B, 5d   Deciding that her life in England was too confining, Englishwoman Mary Kingsley (1862–1900) set out for West Africa where she often traveled by walking and swimming, meeting discomfort, disappointment, and terror along the way.

Exercise 12C, 5   Alejandro Malaspina (1754–1810?), Spanish explorer, led a scientific voyage to the Americas from 1789 to 1790. While conducting studies in Chile and Peru with his crew of scientists, he received new orders from Spain to look for a northern route between the Atlantic and Pacific Oceans. Although he failed to find such a route, on the return trip from Alaska he explored and made the first maps of the northern coast of America.

INTRODUCE Lesson 12

(Book A, page 70)

Remind students that the theme of Lessons 11 and 12 is "Travel."

Display, read, and translate the opening quotation from Lesson 12: *Vade mecum.* "Go with me."

- Ask students if they usually go places alone or with others. (Answers will vary.) When you go places with others, who goes along with you on the journey? (possible answers: parents, friends)
- Point out that *venio,* meaning "to come," and *via,* meaning "journey," are two of the Latin roots in Lesson 12. They tie with the "travel" theme.

PREVIEW Familiar Words

(Book A, pages 71 - 72)

adventure, eventually, telephone, telescope, television

ACTIVITY 1: *venio, ventum*

Display the familiar words *adventure* and *eventually*. Read them orally, pointing at each one, and then chorally with the class. Underline *vent* in each word.

Ask students the following questions:

- What does the word *adventure* suggest to you? (excitement, new things, an incredible experience) Does *adventure* suggest "excitement to come"? (yes)
- Practice makes perfect *eventually*. Is *eventually* "right now," or "in times to come"? ("in times to come")

Ask: What is the shared meaning for *vent* in these words? (to come)

ACTIVITY 2: *tele*

Display the familiar words *telephone, telescope,* and *television*. Read them orally, pointing at each one, and then chorally with the class. Underline *tele* in each word.

Ask students the following questions:

- What does a *telephone* enable you to do? (speak and hear at a distance)
- What does a *telescope* enable you to do? (see at a distance; see things such as planets that are far away)
- What does *television* enable you to do? (see and hear news and entertainment produced at a distant site)

Ask: What is the shared meaning for *tele* in these words? (at a distance)

Review: The familiar words indicate that *vent* suggests "to come," and *tele* suggests "at a distance."

PRESENT Key Words

(Book A, pages 70–73)

Display the Lesson 12 Greek and Latin roots and review their meanings:

- the Latin root *iter, itineris* (*itin*), meaning "journey"
- the Latin root *venio, venire, veni, ventum* (*vent, vene*), meaning "to come"
- the Greek root *tele,* meaning "at a distance"
- the Latin root *via,* meaning "way, street, road, journey"

Have students read the key words chorally: *advent, circumvent, convene, deviate, devious, impervious, intervene, itinerant, itinerary, telepathy.*

Present each of the key words by discussing the following:

- pronunciation
- definitions/connections to the root
- sentences
- parts of speech
- word forms

The *Nota Bene* on page 72 shows some recent derivatives of *tele* (e.g., *telethon* and *telegenic*).

GUIDE Practice

True or False

Have students print TRUE on a piece of green paper, and FALSE on a piece of red paper. Tell them to listen to each key word and sentence that you read aloud, decide whether the sentence is true or false, and mentally select the proper paper.

Then, on a signal from you, they should close their eyes and hold up either TRUE (green paper) or FALSE (red paper). This way, you can prevent copycat answering, and you can tell at a glance which students are correct and incorrect.

1. *Convene.*	To *convene* a meeting is to break it up.		false
2. *Advent.*	Hot weather announces the *advent* of summer.		true
3. *Itinerant.*	*Itinerant* people move frequently.		true
4. *Intervene.*	To *intervene* is to take many trips.		false
5. *Circumvent.*	To *circumvent* a rule is to get around it.		true
6. *Devious.*	It takes a *devious* person to break a lot of rules without getting caught.		true
7. *Impervious.*	Some smokers are *impervious* to their families' requests that they quit.		true
8. *Deviate.*	To *deviate* is to stay on the straight and narrow path.		false
9. *Itinerary.*	An *itinerary* is a list of all the items to be discussed at a meeting.		false
10. *Telepathy.*	*Telepathy* is mind-to-mind communication.		true

Stop and have students defend their answers whenever you see a mix of red and green responses. With the help of the dictionary, teams of students can compose additional true/false sentences in which they use the key words.

Lesson 12 Key Word Activity Master (see page 96)

Answers:

1. C
2. B
3. A
4. E
5. D
6. impervious
7. intervene
8. convene
9. advent
10. circumvent
11. *itinerant* and *itinerary*
12. *devious* and *deviate*
13. *convention* and *intervene*
14. *circumvent* and *advent*

ASSIGN Exercises

(Book A, pages 73–74)

REVIEW Lessons 11 and 12

Display the adjectives and nouns from Lessons 11 and 12 listed below in random order. Have students sort them and arrange them alphabetically, as shown below. Ask such questions as:

- Which adjective usually describes glass? (*translucent*)
- Which adjective usually describes a verb? (*transitive*)
- Which noun usually means "atmosphere" or "environment"? (*ambience*)
- Which noun usually means "a big conference or meeting"? (*convention*)

Then have students study the remaining adjectives and nouns, put combinations together, and write "definition sentences." (possible sentences: *A devious itinerary* is a deceptive travel plan. An *aberrant transgression* is a mistake the person would not be expected to make. *Erratic episodes* are irregular incidents.)

Adjectives	Nouns
aberrant	ambience
devious	convention
erratic	episode
impervious	exodus
transitive	intervention
transitory	itinerary
translucent	obituary
	telepathy
	transgression

SELECT Review Exercises

(Book A, pages 75–76)

LESSON 13

Literary and Historical References

2. celerity

In Greek mythology, Atlanta, huntress and voyager with the Argonauts, challenges each of her suitors to a footrace; losers are put to death, and the winner, Hippomones, becomes her husband. He, however, has tricked her by dropping along the way golden apples that she cannot resist picking up.

3. concur

In *Julius Caesar, Macbeth,* and *Hamlet,* the murder of a head of state or an event related to it occurs simultaneously with an aberration in nature.

4. discourse

With a treatise published in 1543, Polish astronomer Nicolaus Copernicus (1473–1543) explained his belief that the sun is the center of our solar system, with planets, including Earth, revolving around it. He contradicted the belief strongly held at the time that Earth is the center of the universe.

Although denied the formal education accessible to men, Margaret Fuller (1810–1850) read widely, became a journalist, wrote novels, and was a challenging conversationalist on subjects usually reserved for men. She achieved renown for her analysis of the role of women in *Woman in the Nineteenth Century,* published in 1845.

5. incur

As described by ninth-century B.C. poet Homer in *The Odyssey,* Odysseus and his men seek refuge in the cave of the one-eyed giant Polyphemus while on their way back to Ithaca after the Trojan War. By sending him into a stupor with strong wine, Odysseus is able to blind Polyphemus and devise a method of escape: clinging to the underside of rams that the giant sends out to graze.

7. succor

As a nurse, Clara Barton (1821–1912) assisted presidents and organized supplies and services for soldiers in the United States, Europe, and Cuba.

American novelist Louisa May Alcott (1832–1888) drew upon her own experiences in her portrait of Jo March, the eldest of four sisters in *Little Women.*

10. conjecture

Mentioned by Plato (427?–347 B.C.) as an island having a highly developed civilization but destroyed by an earthquake, the legendary Atlantis continues to tantalize scholars and stimulate research to determine if it existed.

Exercise 13B, 2b   In Luke 10:30–37, Christ uses the parable of the Good Samaritan to illustrate loving one's neighbor as oneself. The Samaritan in the parable is the third traveler to pass an injured robbery victim on the roadside but the first to give him aid by tending to his wounds, carrying him to an inn, and caring for him there. Although the Samaritan is traveling in unfriendly territory, he takes the risk of befriending the injured man.

Exercise 13B, 2c   Scotswoman Donaldina Cameron (1869–1968) saved or rescued many girls from slavery or concubinage in the vicinity of San Francisco even as late as the 1930s.

Exercise 13B, 4a   Although the creatures that "roared their terrible roars" in *Where the Wild Things Are* seemed to some parents and reviewers to be frightening to children, the book received the esteemed Caldecott Award in 1984. American author and illustrator Maurice Sendak (b. 1928) says that he tries to draw what children feel: pleasure, suffering, and defenselessness.

Exercise 13B, 6b   The Moors from Morocco introduced Arabic tradition in religion, art, language, and learning to Spain. Although flourishing there for seven centuries, Moors were expelled in the fifteenth century by King Ferdinand and Queen Isabella, who could no longer tolerate Muslim beliefs in solidly Catholic Spain.

INTRODUCE Lesson 13

(Book A, page 77)

Tell students that the theme of Lessons 13 and 14 is "Sports."

Display, read, and translate the opening quotation from Lesson 13: *Tempus ludendi.* "A time for playing."

- Ask students what they do when playing almost any sport. (They run.) What piece of equipment is common to tennis, soccer, football, baseball, and basketball? (ball) In football and basketball, what do players do with the ball? (throw it, catch it)

- Point out that the Latin roots in this lesson relate to *swiftness, running, balls,* and *throwing,* which tie with the theme "Sports."

PREVIEW Familiar Words

(Book A, pages 78–79)

current, cursor, eject, injection

ACTIVITY 1: *curro*

Display the familiar words *current* and *cursor*. Read them orally, pointing at each one, and then chorally with the class. Underline *cur* in each word.

Ask students the following questions:

- What does the *cursor* on your computer do at the end of each line? (It *runs* back to the beginning of the next line.)
- How does "running" connect with *currents*? (Electric currents run through wires. The currents of many mountain streams *run* downhill rapidly.)

Ask: What is the shared meaning for *cur* in these words? (run)

ACTIVITY 2: *jacio, jacere, jeci, jactum*

Display the familiar words, *eject* and *project*. Read them orally, pointing at each one, and then chorally with the class. Underline *ject* in each word.

Ask students the following questions:

- When a plane goes into a nosedive and the pilot *ejects* himself, what does the *ejection* mechanism do? (It *throws* the pilot clear of the plane.)
- When an actor *projects* her voice, what is she doing? (She is making sure that her voice can be heard even in the back of the theater. She is *throwing* her voice into the back row.)

Ask: What is the shared meaning for *ject* in these words? (throw)

Review: The familiar words indicate that *cur* suggests "running," and *ject* suggests "throwing."

PRESENT Key Words

(Book A, pages 77–80)

Display the Lesson 13 Latin roots and review their meanings:

- the Latin root *celer,* meaning "swift "
- the Latin roots *curro, currere, cucurri, cursum* (*cur*), meaning "to run" and *cursor, cursoris* (*cur*), meaning "runner"
- the Latin root *glomus,* meaning "ball"
- the Latin root *jacio, jacere, jeci, jactum* (*ject*), meaning "to throw"

Have students read the key words chorally: *abject, accelerate, celerity, concur, conglomeration, conjecture, discourse, incur, interjection, precursor, succor.*

Present each of the key words by discussing the following:

- pronunciation
- definitions/connections to the root
- sentences
- parts of speech
- word forms

GUIDE Practice

ACTIVITY 1: Where?

Display these key words: *conglomeration, acceleration, celerity, conjecture, interjection, succor, abject, discourse.* Ask students the following "where" questions about the words, and promote discussion of their answers.

1. Where might you find a *conglomeration* of old household items? (possible answers: in the attic, basement, garage, storage unit or wherever else the family stores items they might eventually throw away)

2. Where might you see *acceleration* and *celerity*? (possible answers: at a track meet, at an auto race)

3. Where might you receive *succor* after a disaster? (possible answers: from family, friends, social-service agencies, shelters, the Red Cross)

4. Where might you see *abject* poverty? (possible answers: in war-torn countries, in countries suffering from famine, in some parts of the United States)

5. Where might you carry on a *discourse* about your favorite book? (possible answers: in a book group, with your friends, with a teacher)

6. Where might you hear loud *interjections*? (possible answers: at a pep rally or athletic event, at a surprise party, during an argument)

7. Where do you see people trying to win money by making *conjectures*? (possible answer: on television quiz shows; some answers are just guesses.)

ACTIVITY 2: Words with the "Run" Root

Display the remaining key words: *concur, incur, precursor.* Point out the root *cur* meaning "run" in each word. Ask students:

- Which word means forerunner? (*precursor*)
- Which word relates to opinions running together? (*concur*)
- If you *incur* the wrath of a road-rage driver, might he feel like running over you? (*possibly*)

Lesson 13 Key Word Activity Master (see page 97)

Answers:

1. C
2. D
3. A
4. B
5. *accelerate* and *celerity*
6. *incur* and *discourse*
7. *concurred* and *succor*
8. *conjectures* and *abject*
9. *precursor* and *discourse*

10–12. Answers will vary.

ASSIGN Exercises

(Book A, pages 80–82)

LESSON 14

Literary and Historical References

1. assail The English word quixotic, meaning "visionary," "unrealistic," comes from the behavior and attitudes of Don Quixote, the character made famous by Spanish author Miguel de Cervantes (1547–1616). He is best known for *Don Quixote de la Mancha* (1605), whose title character believes himself designated to seek adventure in the style of outmoded chivalry. Riding his ancient horse, dressed in rusty armor, and accompanied by his servant Sancho Panza, Don Quixote is a ludicrous but endearing character.

3. exult Born in 1927 in North Carolina and raised in Harlem, Althea Gibson caught the eye of tennis champion Alice Marble, who enabled her to break through the color barrier at tennis tournaments held at Forest Hills, New York.

6. convalesce Although recent medical studies cite a rise in cases of tuberculosis, a disease primarily of the lungs, it no longer means inevitable death, as was the case until the twentieth century.

7. avail In more than 100 stories and novels, American author Horatio Alger (1832–1899) assures his readers that even the poorest boys, such as Ragged Dick and Tattered Tom, can rise to riches and respect if they work hard and do good deeds.

9. valor Even when under German arrest with death imminent, Edith Cavell (1865–1915) did not refute the accusation that she had helped Allied soldiers escape imprisonment in Belgium. Her execution followed.

10. evolve German printer Johann Gutenberg (1397?–1468) is considered to be the first European to use movable types in molds.

Exercise 14B, 1b The battle between American and British forces at Fort Ticonderoga came early in the Revolutionary War, which lasted from 1775 to 1783.

Exercise 14B, 1d British-born Jessica Mitford (b. 1917–1995) criticizes the practices of funeral establishments in *The American Way of Death* (1963).

Exercise 14B, 3b On its maiden voyage from England to New York, the British liner Titanic hit an iceberg and sank on April 14–15, 1912 with a loss of 1,517 lives. The fastest ship of the time, it was thought to be virtually invulnerable to accident.

Exercise 14B, 3d The grandfather of Noah and the oldest person in the Bible, Methuselah is mentioned in Genesis 5:27.

Exercise 14B, 4a The mechanical inventions of the Wright brothers, Wilbur (1867–1912) and Orville (1871–1948), evolved from bicycles to gliders to the first power-driven airplane, successfully flown at Kitty Hawk, North Carolina in December 1903.

Exercise 14B, 4b   Charles Darwin (1809–1882) and Alfred Wallace (1823–1913) appeared on the same platform in 1858 to explain the theory of evolution that their identical though independent studies had developed.

Exercise 14B, 4d   German-born physicist Albert Einstein (1879–1955) revised thinking about the physical universe, especially with the theory of relativity.

Exercise 14B, 5a   The properties of gold make it one of the most precious of metals and consequently a challenge to reproduce. Not only is it beautiful; it does not tarnish, and it is highly malleable, able to be beaten or thinned to a fraction of an inch without separating.

Exercise 14B, 5b   In his autobiography *Black Boy* (1944), Richard Wright (1908–1960) describes the impact of realizing the power of words in print. Passionate to read the work of Baltimore journalist H. L. Mencken, Wright prevailed upon a fellow employee to lend him a library card in 1920, a time when library privileges were denied to African Americans in Memphis.

Exercise 14C, 4   In the story by Carlo Lorezzini (1826–1890) the artisan Gepetto carves a puppet named Pinocchio, whose nose grows longer whenever he tells a lie. French novelist Cyrano de Bergerac (1619–1655) became a legend for fighting whenever ridiculed for his long nose. He is the subject of the play *Cyrano de Bergerac* by French dramatist Edmond Rostand (1868–1918).

Exercise 14C, 5   The character of Fanny Flinching leaves the reader breathless with her nonstop talking in the novel by Charles Dickens (1812–1870).

INTRODUCE Lesson 14

(Book A, page 82)

Remind students that the theme of Lessons 13 and 14 is "Sports."

Display, read, and translate the opening quotation from Lesson 14: *Audaces fortuna juvat.* "Fortune favors the bold."

- Ask student how a football player might be bold? (possible answers: He might courageously tackle someone twice his size. He might bravely try to return an intercepted pass even though five opponents are going to jump on him.) If two teams of equal ability meet, but the players on one team are bolder than the players on the other, which team would you favor to win? (The bolder team. As the quotation says, "Fortune favors the bold.")

- Point out that the Latin roots in this lesson relate to *being strong, jumping, revolving, leaping,* all activities that tie with the "Sports" theme.

PREVIEW Familiar Words

(Book A, pages 84)

prevail, valiant, revolve, revolution

ACTIVITY 1: *valeo*

Display the familiar words *prevail* and *valiant*. Read them orally, pointing at each one, and then chorally with the class. Underline *vail* in *prevail*, and *val* in *valiant*.

Ask students the following questions:

- What are the characteristics of a *valiant* person? (strength and courage)
- Which familiar word means "to win, to overcome"? (*prevail*)
- What characteristics do athletes need in order to *prevail* in contests? (skill, endurance, strength)

Ask: What is the shared meaning for *vail* and *val* in these words? (being strong)

ACTIVITY 2: *volvo*

Display the familiar words *revolve* and *revolution*. Read them orally, pointing at each one, and then chorally with the class. Underline *vol* in each word.

Ask students the following questions:

- As the earth rotates on its axis, we experience day and night. Which familiar word is a synonym for *rotate*? (*revolve*)
- How many *revolutions* around the sun does the earth make in a year? (one) In this context, does *revolution* mean "spin" or "revolve in an orbit or a circle"? (revolve in an orbit or a circle)
- Is there another meaning for *revolution*? (yes, an uprising, a revolt against the government) During this type of revolution, is there often so much disorder that things seem to be "spinning and going around in circles"? (yes)

Ask: What is the shared meaning for *vol* in these words? (revolve, spin, go around in circles)

Review: The familiar words indicate that *val* and *vail* suggest "strength," and *volve* suggests "revolving."

PRESENT Key Words

(Book A, pages 82–85)

Display the Lesson 14 Latin roots and review their meanings

- the Latin root *salio, salire, salui, saltum* (*sal, sil*), meaning "to jump, to leap"
- the Latin root *valeo, valere, valui, valitum* (*val, vail*), meaning "to be strong"
- the Latin root *volvo* (*vol*), meaning "to revolve"

Have students read the key words chorally: *assail, avail, convalesce, desultory, evolve, exult, prevalent, resilient, salient, valor, voluble.*

Present each of the key words by discussing the following:

- pronunciation
- definitions/connections to the root
- sentences
- parts of speech
- word forms

GUIDE Practice

Context Activity

Tell students that the passage you are going to read aloud contains most of the key words from Lesson 14. They should simply listen to your first and second oral readings of the passage to get an idea of the intent and content. During your third reading, pause at the end of each sentence. Ask students to define the underlined word. Context should help students come up with definitions similar to those that appear after the passage.

Passage for oral reading:

Squeeky the cat feared nothing; he was valorous.
Although dogs were prevalent in the neighborhood, he was not concerned.
He availed himself of secret pathways when he was roaming the neighborhood.

One day, an assailant jumped out at him in an alley.
The big dog's most salient feature was his bright blue eyes.
Squeeky was not desultory in defending himself with his sharp claws.
At first the dog was resilient and bounced back.
But finally he ran away so that he could convalesce.

Squeeky was voluble in telling the neighborhood cats about the battle.
With each retelling, his story evolved into a more heroic tale.
Squeeky exulted in his victory.

Probable definitions of underlined words

valorous:	brave
prevalent:	usual
availed:	supplied herself, to her advantage
assailant:	attacker
salient:	conspicuous
desultory:	slow
resilient:	recovering quickly
convalesce:	heal his wounds
voluble:	talkative
evolved:	developed
exulted:	rejoiced

Lesson 14 Key Word Activity Master (see page 98)

Answers:

1. exultant
2. assailing
3. resilient
4. desultory
5. B
6. D
7. E
8. A
9. C
10. F
11. "To no avail" often means "unsuccessfully."
12. Answers will vary. Point out that some valorous acts might be performed off the athletic field, e.g., jumping to save a child about to be hit by a car.

ASSIGN Exercises

(Book A, pages 85–87)

REVIEW Lessons 13 and 14

Display in random order the key words from Lessons 13 and 14 shown below. Remind students that the theme of these lessons is "Sports." In terms of sports and physical activity, which words are positive and which are negative?

Have students defend their listings, since a word like *convalescence* could be negative in terms of "getting injured and needing time to heal" but positive in terms of "recovery."

Possible/probable listings

Positive Words	Negative Words
acceleration	abject
celerity	convalescence
exult	desultory
resilient	voluble (too much negative talk)
valor	assailant

interjections (cheers)

Tell students that the passage you are going to read aloud contains most of the key words from Lesson 14. They should simply listen to your first and second oral readings of the passage to get an idea of the intent and content. During your third reading, pause at the end of each sentence. Ask students to define the underlined word. Context should help students come up with definitions similar to those that appear after the passage.

Passage for oral reading

The <u>discourse</u> between the player and the umpire was not at all friendly.

From the <u>conglomeration</u> of equipment, the player had picked a rigged bat.

The player put forth his <u>conjecture</u> that the bat met the regulations.

He argued to no <u>avail</u>.

The umpire did not <u>concur</u>.

His <u>salient</u> characteristic was stubbornness.

The player <u>incurred</u> the wrath of this umpire by arguing with him.

The argument <u>evolved</u> into a shouting match.

The player's teammates gave him no <u>succor</u>.

They knew that the <u>prevailing</u> opinion was, "The umpire is always right."

Probable definitions of underlined words

discourse:	conversation
conglomeration:	piles, assortment
conjecture:	opinion
avail:	benefit, advantage
voncur:	agree
salient:	most prominent
incurred:	brought upon himself
evolved:	grew and developed
wuccor:	help
prevailing:	common, accepted

SELECT Review Exercises

(Book A, pages 87–88)

LESSON 15

Literary and Historical References

5. canine
Rin Tin Tin, an ex-German Army dog, first appeared in the film *Where the North Begins* (1923), which was followed by other films and serials until 1930. The collie Lassie (actually a laddie named Pal) took title billing in *Lassie Come Home* (1942), based on a novel by Eric Knight. Production of Lassie films continued until 1962, along with television and cartoon series.

6. caper
Mr. Toad of Toad Hall, along with his companions Mole, Water Rat, and Badger, finds adventure along the river Thames in *The Wind in the Willows* by English author Kenneth Grahame (1859–1932).

7. caprice
In the comic strip *Peanuts,* American cartoonist Charles Schulz (1922–2000) created characters who engage in perpetual one-upmanship. These include Lucy, Linus, Peppermint Patty, and the perennial victim Charlie Brown.

9. equine
French artist Rosa Bonheur (1822–1899) was the best known painter of animals in the nineteenth century.

11. equestrian
Robyn Smith (b. 1944) claimed the title of Best American Jockey from 1972 to 1978.

Exercise 15B, 1d
Emperor Charlemagne (742–814) held dominion over Frankish territory and as Emperor of the West (800–814) controlled a vast realm in what is now Europe. The painting of Mona Lisa by Leonardo da Vinci (1452–1519) is probably the most familiar piece of art on exhibition in the Louvre Museum in Paris.

Exercise 15B, 2b
Although Odysseus is disguised as a beggar, his old dog Argos recognizes his master after twenty years of absence during and after the Trojan War. Epic poet Homer lets the dog die moments later of old age and excitement.

Exercise 15B, 2c
Barbara Woodhouse (1910–1988) was so successful in explaining dog-training methods that her classes were filmed for television. Besides having the pleasure of watching dogs learn to behave, viewers appreciated Woodhouse's sensitivity to animals and her no-nonsense advice to ignorant or over-indulgent owners.

Exercise 15B, 3c	*Gone With the Wind* (1936) became a best-seller and the film (1939) starring Vivien Leigh, Clark Gable, and Leslie Howard was one of the most popular in movie history. American author Margaret Mitchell (1900–1949) had not taken her manuscript seriously; it reached an editor's desk only because of the enthusiasm of a friend.
Exercise 15C, 3	So-called killer bees are a strain released accidentally in South America where scientists in the 1950s were engaged in experiments. Advancing northward through Central America, Mexico, and into the United States, these insects are troublesome to human beings because of their severe stings and their displacement of native bees.
Exercise 15C, 4	Fictional horses Black Beauty and Black Stallion became the subjects of two well-known series, the first the work of Anna Sewell (1820–1878) and the second that of Walter Farley (1915–1989).

INTRODUCE Lesson 15

(Book A, page 89)

Tell students that the theme of Lessons 15 and 16 is "Animals."

Display, read, and translate the opening quotation from Lesson 15: *Ubi mel, ubi apes.* "Where there is honey, there are bees."

- Ask students to restate the quotation, substituting other words for *honey* and *bees.* (possible answers: Where there is a *beach,* there are *sunbathers.* Where there is *smoke,* there is *fire.*)
- Point out that the Latin roots in this lesson relate to *bee, bird, cow, ox, dog, goat,* and *horse,* all of which tie with the theme "Animals."

PREVIEW Familiar Words

(Book A, pages 90–91)

aviation, aviator, Capricorn

ACTIVITY 1: *avis*

Display the familiar words *aviator* and *aviation.* Read them orally, pointing at each one, and then chorally with the class. Underline avi in each word.

Ask students the following questions:

- Where does *aviation* take place? (in the air, in flight)
- What does an *aviator* do? (flies a plane)

Ask: What is the shared meaning for *avi* in these words? (flight)

ACTIVITY 2: *caper, capra*

Display the familiar word, *Capricorn.* Read it orally, pointing at it, and then chorally with the class. Underline *capr* in the word.

Ask students the following questions:

- What is a constellation? (a group of stars, often named after the shape they suggest in outline)
- What animal does the constellation *Capricorn* suggest in outline? (a goat)

Review: The familiar words indicate that *avi* suggests "flight" (derived from *bird*) and *capr* suggests a derivation from *goat.*

PRESENT Key Words

(Book A, pages 89–92)

Display the Lesson 15 Latin roots and review their meanings:

- the Latin root *apis,* meaning "bee"
- the Latin root *avis,* meaning "bird"
- the Latin root *bos, bovis,* meaning "cow, ox"
- the Latin root *canis,* meaning "dog"
- the Latin root *caper, capra,* meaning "goat"
- the Latin root *equus,* meaning "horse"

Have students read the key words chorally: *apiary, aviary, bovine, canine, caper, caprice, capricious, equestrian, equine, equitation.*

Present each of the key words by discussing the following:

- pronunciation
- definitions/connections to the root
- sentences
- parts of speech
- word forms

The *Nota Bene* on page 90 makes reference to children's canine teeth.

GUIDE Practice

ACTIVITY 1: The playful words

Display the key words *caprice, caper, capricious*. Explain that these three words have less to do with "goats" than with "playfulness." What relationship to students see between goats and being playful?

- Ask the part(s) of speech of each word. (*caprice:* noun. *caper:* verb or noun. *capricious:* adjective.)
- Display in random order the synonyms of these three words, shown below. Have students sort the synonyms and match them with the words, as follows:

  > *caprice:* whim, impulse, change of mind
  > *caper:* skip, hop, leap, frolic
  > *capricious:* changeable, fickle, undependable, playful

ACTIVITY 2: The *flight*-connected words

Display the key words *aviary* and *apiary*. Point out that only one letter is different in the two words. They are both connected with flight since both birds and bees fly. But which is which? (*aviary:* birds. *apiary:* bees)

ACTIVITY 3: The animal-connected words

Display the key words *canine, bovine, equine, equestrian, equitation*. Ask students these questions:

- Which three are related to horses? (*equine, equestrian, equitation*) Which of those three words is a person? (*equestrian*) Which is the art of horsemanship? (*equitation*)
- Which word pertains to wolves as well as dogs? (*canine*)
- Which word pertains to cattle? (*bovine.*) Are oxen as well as cows heavy, slow, unintelligent animals? (yes)

Lesson 15 Key Word Activity Master (see page 99)

Answers:

1. C
2. G
3. A
4. B
5. F
6. E
7. H
8. D
9. C
10. B
11. D
12. A
13. Answers will vary.
14. Since the equestrian might be a bareback rider, she would be most likely to be hired to perform in the circus. The others are not performers.

ASSIGN Exercises

(Book A, pages 92–93)

LESSON 16

Literary and Historical References

1. feline
The Broadway musical *Cats* is based on poems written by T. S. Eliot (1888–1965), American-born poet, playwright, and literary critic.

3. lionize
Anthony Trollope (1815–1882) was one of several English writers who drew a large audience when they came to the United States to read from their work.

5. porcine
Miss Piggy is one of the many "Muppets" of American puppeteer Jim Henson (1936–1990), who was also the designer of Big Bird, Kermit the Frog, and Cookie Monster.

Exercise 16B, 1d
Writing under the pen name of George Orwell, Eric Blair (1903–1950) used fiction such as *Animal Farm* to highlight the dangers of revolution leading to totalitarian regimes such as that which occurred in Russia in 1917 and in Germany, Italy, and Spain in the 1930s. Orwell's novel *1984* envisions the consequences of the loss of individual freedom if Big Brother and Newspeak were to become a reality.

Exercise 16B, 2c
Thoroughly greased for her English Channel swim in 1926, Gertrude Ederle (1906–2003) set a record of fourteen hours and thirteen minutes even though bad weather forced her to swim thirty-five miles instead of the twenty-one miles separating France and England.

Exercise 16B, 2d
Although English writer Izaak Walton (1593–1683) was primarily a biographer, he is best known for his fishing expertise.

Exercise 16B, 3b
In an untitled poem about meeting a snake, American poet Emily Dickinson (1830–1886) says that for several of nature's creatures she feels a "transport of cordiality": "But never met this Fellow/Attended, or alone/Without a tighter breathing/And Zero at the bone."

Exercise 16B, 4b
The bear Winnie the Pooh, Piglet, and the donkey Eeyore figure in the children's book by English writer, A. A. Milne (1882–1956).

Exercise 16B, 5c
The Beatles, a British rock group that became a musical phenomenon in 1962, were John Lennon, George Harrison, Paul McCartney, and Ringo Starr. Members of the original Supremes were Diana Ross, Mary Birdsong, Florence Ballard, and Mary Wilson.

Exercise 16B, 6a
Jane Goodall (b. 1934) describes her studies of chimpanzees in several books, one of which is *My Friends, the Wild Chimpanzees* (1967). In *Gorillas in the Mist,* published in 1983, Dian Fossey (1932–1985) gives an account of her fifteen years in Africa studying gorilla habits and habitats.

Exercise 16B, 6d   With the publication of *On the Origin of Species* in 1859, Charles Darwin (1809–1882) prepared the way for controversy about the origins of human life. Several distinguished scientists supported Darwin's contention that humans and other primates evolved from a common ancestor, an idea that shocked believers in God's creation of Adam and Eve as described in the first chapter of Genesis.

INTRODUCE Lesson 16

(Book A, page 94)

Remind students that the theme of Lessons 15 and 16 is "Animals."

Display, read, and translate the opening quotation from Lesson 16: *In pacem leones, in proelio cervi.* "Be lions in peace; be deer in battle."

- Ask students about the characteristics of lions. (possible answers: strength, courage) Ask about the characteristics of deer. (possible answers: speed, skill in evading the hunter) Why does the quotation advise being lions in peace and deer in battle? (speed of movement is an advantage in a battle; a strong, kingly, courageous attitude is an advantage in times of peace)
- Point out that the Latin and Greek roots in this lesson relate to *cat, lion, fish, swine, pig, hog, serpent, snake, monkey, ape, bear, animal,* all of which tie with the "Animals" theme.

PREVIEW Familiar Words

(Book A, pages 94 and 95)

lion, lioness, lionhearted, pork

ACTIVITY 1: *leo*

Display the familiar words *lion, lioness,* and *lionhearted*. Read them orally, pointing at each one, and then chorally with the class.

Ask students the following questions:

- Which familiar word is a female animal? (*lioness*)
- Which familiar word is the king of the beasts? (*lion*)
- What does *lionhearted* mean? (courageous, as brave and kingly as a lion)

Ask: What animal is associated most strongly with kingship and courage? (lion)

ACTIVITY 2: *porcus*

Display the familiar word *pork*. Read it orally, pointing at it, and then chorally with the class.

Ask students the following questions:

- Have you ever eaten a pork chop or a pork roast? (At least a few students will probably answer yes.)
- From what animal did this meat come? (a pig)

Ask: What is the derivation of the word *pork*? (The Latin root *porcus* meaning "swine, pig, hog.")

Review: The familiar words indicate that lion-related words suggest "strength," and that the word *pork* is derived from *porcus*, and has a connection with swine or pigs.

PRESENT Key Words

(Book A, pages 94–96)

Display the Lesson 16 Greek and Latin roots and review their meanings

- the Latin root *felis*, meaning "cat"
- the Latin root *leo, leonis* and the Greek root *leon*, meaning "lion"
- the Latin root *piscis*, meaning "fish"
- the Latin root *porcus*, meaning "swine, pig, hog"
- the Latin root *serpens, serpentis*, meaning "serpent, snake"
- the Latin root *simia*, meaning "monkey, ape"
- the Latin root *ursa*, meaning "bear"
- the Greek root *zoion, zoa* (*zoo*), meaning "living being, animal"

Have students read the key words chorally: *feline, leonine, lionize, piscine, porcine, serpentine, simian, ursine, zoology.*

Present each of the key words by discussing the following:

- pronunciation
- definitions/connections to the root
- sentences
- parts of speech
- word forms

GUIDE Practice

ACTIVITY 1: Animal Names

Tell students you are going to say some proper names for animals. Have them guess the kind of animal that would have each name.

Porky: pig

Serpentina: snake

Leo: lion

Felicity: cat

Ursula: bear

Simi: monkey

Zooey: human being who wants to be a zoologist

ACTIVITY 2: Animal-like Behavior

Point out that people are sometimes said to behave like animals. Tell students to listen to each of your sentences and decide whether it is using animal-related words to praise or to blame. Have them explain their answers.

- She showed *leonine* courage in protecting her baby. (Praise. She was brave as a lion.)
- She moves with *feline* grace. (Praise. She moves as smoothly as a cat.)
- His table manners are *porcine*. (Blame. He eats like a pig.)
- He left the campsite looking as if it had had *ursine* visitors. (Blame. He did not clean up. The campsite looked as if bears had trampled through it.)
- The author did not want to be *lionized* just because her book had been made into a movie. (Praise. She remained modest. She did not want to be treated like a celebrity, like the royal queen of the beasts.)
- He steered the boat through every twist in the *serpentine* mountain stream. (Praise. The river slithered downhill like a serpent, but he did not lose control of the boat.)
- The parents laughed at their son's imitation of *simian* behavior when the little boy thumped his chest. (Praise. The little boy entertained them by acting like a monkey.)
- Olympic swimmers have a love of the water that is positively *piscine*. (Praise. Water is their element. They swim like fish.)

Lesson 16 Key Word Activity Master (see page 100)

Answers:

1. porcine
2. piscine
3. simian
4. ursine
5. piscine
6. simian
7. porcine
8. feline
9. feline
10. porcine
11. ursine
12. simian
13. serpentine
14. leonine
15. zoology
16. lionize

ASSIGN Exercises

(Book A, pages 96–98)

REVIEW Lessons 15 and 16

Display in random order the words grouped below. Have students sort these animal-related words from Lessons 15 and 16 into three groups, as shown.

Words Related to Farm Animals	Related to Wild Creatures	Related to Pets
bovine	leonine	canine (can also be related to wild creatures)
equine	serpentine	feline (can also be related to wild creatures)
porcine	simian	piscine (can also be related to wild creatures)
	ursine	

Display in random order the words grouped below. Have students sort these key words from Lessons 15 and 16 into three groups, as shown.

Words Related to Horses	Related to the Playfulness of Goats	Related to Flight
equine	caper	apiary
equitation	caprice	aviary
equestrian	capricious	

SELECT Review Exercises

(Book A, pages 98–99)

Lesson 1 Key Word Activity Master

Name _____ **Date** _____

Find the answer for each rhyming riddle. Write its letter in the blank.

1. ____ What do you call one pig's speech?

2. ____ What do you call a legend about one huge stone?

3. ____ What do you call an initial of a creature with a shell?

4. ____ What do you call looking at a division into two parts?

A. clam *monogram*

B. hog *monologue*

C. *bisection* inspection

D. *monolith* myth

Match these parts to make four words, then write one word in each blank.

uni	cycle
bi	lateral

5. _____ 7. _____

6. _____ 8. _____

Write the four words from exercises 5–8 in this paragraph, deciding which is the best word for each.

I wanted to make a (9) _____ decision on my own about

what kind of bike to buy. My choice was a one-wheeled (10) _____.

But decisions in my family are (11) _____ since Mom pays the

bills. She and I ended up getting a (12) _____.

On each line, write the word that the clue brings to mind.

bipartisan	*duplex*	*duplicate*	*monopolize*	*monarch*	*unanimous*

13. one royal crown _____

14. everyone agreed _____

15. two political parties _____

16. two front doors _____

17. identical twins _____

18. one student doing all the talking in a class discussion _____

Lesson 2 Key Word Activity Master

Name _____ **Date** _____

1. Use a clue from part of the word *trio*. How many people in a *triumvirate*?

   _____

2. Use a clue from part of the word *quarter*. How many people in a *quartet*?

   _____

3. Use a clue from part of the word *centipede*. How many years for a *centenary*

   celebration? _____

4. Use a clue from part of the word *triplet*. How many books in a *trilogy*?

   _____

5. Use a clue from part of the word *century*. How many years in a *centennial*?

   _____

On each line, write the word that the clue brings to mind.

trisect	*quatrain*	*decathlon*	*centigrade*	*quadrant*	*decimate*

6. competing in ten events _____

7. dividing into four parts _____

8. cutting into three parts _____

9. massive destruction _____

10. a thermometer scale _____

11. four rhyming lines _____

Match the words in the two columns. In each blank, write the letter of the best match.

12. ____ quartet   A. leaders

13. ____ triumvirate   B. singers

14. ____ decathlon   C. poets

15. ____ quatrain   D. athletes

16. ____ trilogy   E. authors

Lesson 3 Key Word Activity Master

Name _____ **Date** _____

Find the answer for each rhyming riddle. Write its letter in the blank.

1. ____ What is an evergreen tree that wants to be alone?
2. ____ What is a teenager who's always hanging around?
3. ____ What do you call a place of seclusion for seafood?
4. ____ What do you call an eighty-year-old dictator?
5. ____ What is an uproar on the planet Pluto?
6. ____ What do you call a cure-all notion?

A. *omnipresent* adolescent
B. spruce *recluse*
C. *totalitarian* octogenarian
D. oyster *cloister*
E. *panacea* idea
F. Plutonian *pandemonium*

Find the word for the blank inside the underlined word.

7. In a <u>totalitarian</u> government, one person holds _ _ _ _ _ control.

8. An <u>omnipresent</u> fragrance is always _ _ _ _ _ _ _ at the perfume counter.

9. From inside the <u>closet</u>, she said, "Don't _ _ _ _ _ the door."

10. An <u>omnipotent</u> ruler is a _ _ _ _ _ _ threat to the rights of citizens.

On each line write the word that the clue brings to mind.

omnivorous	*preclude*	*holocaust*	*catholic*

11. consuming all _____

12. destroying all _____

13. preventing all _____

14. including all _____

Lesson 4 Key Word Activity Master

Name _____ **Date** _____

Find the answer for each rhyming riddle. Write its letter in the blank.

1. ____ What to you call a stuck-up conceited choo-choo?

2. ____ What do you call being extremely conceited?

3. ____ What could be the motto of peace lovers?

4. ____ What do you call the destruction of a country?

5. ____ What do you call a clear and open warning signal?

6. ____ What do you call an outlaw who earns a salary?

7. ____ What do you call a grown-up doorway?

8. ____ What do you call a fragrance that is just beginning?

A. *vanity* insanity

B. *vain* train

C. *negate* hate

D. *overt* alert

E. nation *annihilation*

F. mature *aperture*

G. paid *renegade*

H. *incipient* scent

9. Would you welcome the *inception* of a dancing class in your school? Why or why not?

_____

_____

10. What person do you most admire for deservedly *vaunted* achievements? Why?

_____

_____

11. What is the most *vacuous* program you have seen on television? In what way was it empty of content or value?

_____

_____

12. Who do you think was the most *nihilistic* person in history? What negative things did this person do?

_____

_____

Lesson 5 Key Word Activity Master

Name _____ **Date** _____

Match the underlined words with their definitions.

1. ____ satiates   A. do as told

2. ____ replete   B. fills you up

3. ____ comply   C. complete

4. ____ implements   D. become less

5. ____ diminish   E. knives and forks

On each line, write the word that the clue brings to mind.

| *tenuous* | *minutia* | *minuscule* | *microcosm* | *microbe* | *expletive* |

6. It can make you sick. _____

7. It's trivial stuff. _____

8. It's a small world. _____

9. It's thin and flimsy. _____

10. It's very small. _____

11. It's not a polite word. _____

Lesson 6 Key Word Activity Master

Name _____ **Date** _____

On each line, write the word that the clue brings to mind.

polygon	magnanimity	megaphone	polygamy	macrocosm	megalomania

1. so many mates _____

2. so many sides _____

3. so much noise _____

4. so much size _____

5. so much generosity _____

6. so much self-importance _____

In each sentence circle the two words that have the same root.

7. The magnitude of the project impressed the magnate who ran the company.

8. His copying machine used copious amounts of paper.

9. The rich magnate made magnanimous gifts to charity.

10. The jeweled box for my magnifying glass is a magnificent container.

Complete exercises 11 and 12 with a partner.

11. Name someone from history who might be considered a *megalomaniac*. Explain.

    _____

    _____

12. Name someone from history who might be considered a *magnate*. Explain.

    _____

    _____

Lesson 7 Key Word Activity Master

Name _____ **Date** _____

Write _Y_ or _N_ for _yes_ or _no_ in the blank before the sentences to answer each question.

1. ____ Did Romeo and Juliet feel that they were _predestined_ for each other?

2. ____ The _vanguard_ of the student council supported an _avant-garde_ school uniform. Did the school leaders want to dress in wild new fashions?

3. ____ The students made a preemptive strike: they shared the information with the teacher committee on their own. Did the students wait to be asked for the information?

4. ____ In the sentence, "Students learn from their teacher," is the noun students the _antecedent_ of the pronoun their?

On each line write the word that the clue brings to mind.

| _precept_ | _preposterous_ | _anterior_ | _premonition_ | _antebellum_ | _pretentious_ |

5. stuck-up and pompous _____

6. a feeling that something bad will happen _____

7. in times past when ladies wore long hoopskirts _____

8. a forward position _____

9. outrageously silly _____

10. a rule for good conduct _____

Find the answer for each rhyming riddle. Write its letter in the blank.

11. ____ What do you call a snake that tells the future?   A. a kept _precept_

12. ____ What do you call a rule that is obeyed?   B. a boa constrictor _predictor_

13. ____ What do you call a marcher who walks ahead of the drum major?   C. an _avant-garde_ yard

14. ____ What do you call a lawn that is ahead of the times?   D. a leader _preceder_

15. ____ What do you call a tough front line of leaders?   E. a hard _vanguard_

Lesson 8 Key Word Activity Master

Name _____ **Date** _____

Fill in the best word (or words) for each line.

| *primeval* | *prime* | *posthumous* | *primordial* | *premier* | *posterior* |

1. after death: _____

2. back or rear: _____

3. two words for *very old*: _____ and _____

4. two words for *first in quality and importance*: _____ and _____

Find the answer for each rhyming riddle. Write its letter in the blank.

5. ____ What do you call a beloved leader?   A. prime time

6. ____ What do you call a tardy monkey?   B. inferior posterior

7. ____ What do you call the best hours of TV?   C. late primate

8. ____ What is the opposite of a superior front?   D. dear premier

9. What are your hopes for *posterity*?

_____

_____

10. Would you like to have lived in *primeval* times? Why or why not?

_____

_____

11. Would you like to be a member of a *premier* team? Why or why not?

_____

_____

12. What is your favorite *prime* time program? At what time do you watch it?

_____

_____

Lesson 9 Key Word Activity Master

Name _____ **Date** _____

In each sentence, circle the two words that have the same root.

1. The artisan used artifice to get outrageous prices for his woodcarvings.

2. People of long ago depicted their ideas in pictographs.

3. He recanted the belief in magical incantations that he had expressed earlier.

4. A writer might express enthusiasm with a rhapsody, and deep feeling with an ode.

5. She showed artless admiration for the primitive artifacts.

Match the columns. In each blank, write the letter of the best match

6. ____ chant   A. parody

7. ____ paint   B. recant

8. ____ praise   C. rhapsodize

9. ____ take back   D. depict

10. ____ mimic   E. incantation

Reread the parodies on page 53 of your book. They mimic well-known poems. Many parodies mimic nursery rhymes like _Humpty Dumpty, Jack and Jill,_ or _Mary Had a Little Lamb._ On the lines below, write a parody of one of these three rhymes.

_____

_____

_____

_____

_____

_____

Lesson 10 Key Word Activity Master

Name _____ **Date** _____

Find the answer for each rhyming riddle. Write its letter in the blank.

1. ____ What do you call a calmed-down leader?

2. ____ What do you call a fully-stocked pantry?

3. ____ What do you call a decoration that swings with ease?

4. ____ What do you call a place for the activities of royalty?

5. ____ What do you call a group in favor of minus signs?

A. nobility *facility*

B. subtraction *faction*

C. *mollified* guide

D. *accrued* food

E. *facile* tassel

On each line write the word that the clue brings to mind.

| *mollify* | *facilitate* | *facsimile* | *crescendo* |

6. make it easy _____

7. make someone take it easy _____

8. make it louder _____

9. make an exact copy _____

Match the words in the two columns. In each blank, write the letter of the best match.

10. ____ efficacious

11. ____ beneficence

12. ____ faculty

13. ____ accrual

14. ____ faction

A. teachers

B. effective

C. clique

D. benefit

E. increase

Lesson 11 Key Word Activity Master

Name _____ Date _____

Find the answer for each rhyming riddle. Write its letter in the blank.

1. ____ What do you call radio noise that jumps from loud to soft?

2. ____ What do you call a mom who somersaults across the street?

3. ____ What do you call fifteen minutes of fame?

4. ____ What do you call a frightening biography of a person who died?

5. ____ What do you call a mischievous look?

A. *transitory* glory

B. *transgression* expression

C. *aberrant* parent

D. *erratic* static

E. scary *obituary*

In each sentence, circle the two words that have the same root.

6. When the dog was sick, his behavior was erratic and aberrant.

7. It is a grammar transgression to omit an object for a transitive verb.

8. Many exciting episodes occurred during the exodus of the refugees.

9. His newspaper obituary mentioned the pleasant ambience of his home.

10. The transient tenants took only a transitory interest in their apartments.

On each line, write the word that fits best.

| *aberration* | *episode* | *exodus* | *transients* | *ambience* |

11. A mass of people left the country as a group. _____

12. It was not normal. _____

13. They stayed briefly and moved on. _____

14. It was one chapter of a book. _____

15. Visitors get a sense of history in Washington, DC. _____

Lesson 12 Key Word Activity Master

Name _____ Date _____

Find the answer for each rhyming riddle. Write its letter in the blank.

1. ____ What do you call a gathering of stressed people?

2. ____ What do you call a mishap upon arrival?

3. ____ What do you call a happy travel plan?

4. ____ What do you call a place where you turn aside?

5. ____ What do you call lack of interest in mental communication?

A. merry *itinerary*

B. *advent* accident

C. tension *convention*

D. *telepathy* apathy

E. *deviation* station

On each line, write the word that the clue brings to mind.

intervene	*impervious*	*convene*	*circumvent*	*advent*

6. cannot come through _____

7. can come between _____

8. come together for a meeting _____

9. coming into being, arrival _____

10. come upon a way to get around something _____

In each sentence, circle the two words that have the same root.

11. Itinerant people of long ago did not write an itinerary for their travels.

12. He was sneaky and devious in suggesting that we deviate from the plan.

13. At the convention the chairperson had to intervene to settle arguments.

14. Efforts to circumvent the chairperson caused the advent of hostility.

Lesson 13 Key Word Activity Master

Name _____ **Date** _____

Find the answer for each rhyming riddle. Write its letter in the blank.

1. ____ What do you call fondness for exclamations?

2. ____ What do you call a formal talk about guesswork?

3. ____ What do you call a place for speeding up?

4. ____ What do you call a party given when one big business buys many small businesses?

A. *acceleration* station

B. *conglomeration* celebration

C. *interjection* affection

D. *conjecture* lecture

In each sentence, circle the two words that have the same root.

5. The car salesman said, "This high-speed model will accelerate with celerity."

6. One way to incur boredom is to listen to a long discourse by a dull speaker.

7. The officials concurred that succor should be given to the earthquake victims.

8. He had very little evidence to support his conjectures about abject poverty.

9. As a humorous precursor to his serious discourse, he told a funny story.

10. What *interjections* do you use when you are surprised? Happy? Upset?

_____

_____

11. Do you favor making an outline as a *precursor* to writing a report? Why or why not?

_____

_____

12. On what topics do you *concur* with your friends? On what topics do you disagree?

_____

_____

Lesson 14 Key Word Activity Master

Name _____ **Date** _____

On each line, write the *jumping*-related word that fits best.

resilient	assailing	desultory	exultant

1. jumping for joy _____

2. jumping to attack _____

3. jumping back to original shape _____

4. jumping from one thing to another _____

Match the words in the two columns. In each blank, write the letter of the best match.

5. ____ strong, brave   A. prevalence

6. ____ regaining strength   B. valorous

7. ____ noticeable   C. volubility

8. ____ wide usage   D. convalescing

9. ____ chatter   E. salient

10. ____ develop   F. evolve

11. Some athletes try to break records, to no *avail.* Explain the expression "to no avail."

_____

_____

12. Describe an act of *valor* that you saw an athlete perform.

_____

_____

Lesson 15 Key Word Activity Master

Name _____ **Date** _____

Find the answer for each rhyming riddle. Write its letter in the blank.

1. ____ What do you call the backbone of a horse?

2. ____ What do you call a journalism prank?

3. ____ What do you call cord for tying up dogs?

4. ____ What do you call a dull tree?

5. ____ What do you call the whim of an officer?

6. ____ What is a bird house that does not move?

7. ____ What is a place where beehives are buried?

8. ____ What are the bone-like growths coming out from the head of a goat?

A. *canine* twine

B. *bovine* pine

C. *equine* spine

D. *Capricorn's* horns

E. stationary *aviary*

F. police *caprice*

G. newspaper *caper*

H. *apiary* cemetery

Match the words in the two columns. In each blank, write the letter of the best match.

9. ____ cowboy

10. ____ beekeeper

11. ____ dentist

12. ____ bird keeper

A. aviarist

B. apiarist

C. equitation

D. canines

13. If you had to take care of an animal, what type of animal would you choose: *bovine*, *canine*, or *equine*? Explain your choice.

_____

_____

14. Who is most likely to be hired to perform in the circus: an *apiarist*, an *equestrian*, or an *aviarist*? Explain your answer.

_____

_____

Lesson 16 Key Word Activity Master

Name _____ **Date** _____

Zoologists study creatures that belong to all these groups:

| simian | porcine | piscine | feline | ursine |

Beside the name of each creature, write the group to which it belongs.

1. pig _____

2. shark _____

3. chimpanzee _____

4. grizzly _____

5. guppy _____

6. gorilla _____

7. hog _____

8. jaguar _____

9. kitten _____

10. swine _____

11. polar bear _____

12. monkey _____

On each line write the word that the clue brings to mind.

| leonine | zoology | lionize | serpentine |

13. winding _____

14. fierce _____

15. science related to animal forms _____

16. treating someone like a celebrity _____

Answers to Exercises

LESSON 1

EXERCISE 1A

1. b
2. e
3. b
4. d
5. e
6. b
7. a
8. b
9. c

EXERCISE 1B

1. c
2. d
3. c
4. a
5. a
6. b

EXERCISE 1C

1. monarch
2. monologue
3. monogram
4. unanimous
5. unilateral
6. bilateral
7. bipartisan
8. duplex

LESSON 2

EXERCISE 2A

1. a
2. a
3. d
4. b
5. e
6. d
7. e

EXERCISE 2B

1. trilogy
2. triumvirate
3. quartet
4. quatrain
5. decathlon
6. centigrade
7. bicentennial

EXERCISE 2C

1. *Trilogy*
2. decathlon
3. quatrain
4. trisect(ed)
5. quadrant
6. triumvirate
7. bicentennial
8. quartet
9. decimate(d)

REVIEW EXERCISES FOR LESSONS 1 AND 2

1. *monos, unus*
2. c
3. b
4. c
5. *duo, bi*
6. a. three-sided
   b. cut in four pieces
   c. 1000-year anniversary
   d. in 100 identical copies
   e. three-fold or a house for three families

LESSON 3

EXERCISE 3A
1. a
2. a
3. b
4. e
5. a
6. c
7. c
8. e
9. b

EXERCISE 3B
1. b
2. a
3. c
4. c

EXERCISE 3C
1. panacea
2. recluse
3. holocaust
4. omnipotence
5. pandemonium
6. cloister(ed)
7. omnipresent

LESSON 4

EXERCISE 4A
1. c
2. e
3. e
4. d
5. c
6. c

EXERCISE 4B
1. d
2. d
3. d
4. b

EXERCISE 4C
1. annihilate(d)
2. vaunt
3. inception
4. overt
5. aperture
6. nihilist
7. incipient
8. renegade

REVIEW EXERCISES FOR LESSONS 3 AND 4
1. *pan, omnis*
2. d
3. c
4. c
5. *vanus, vacuus*
6. to deny

LESSON 5

EXERCISE 5A

1. b
2. b
3. b
4. d
5. e
6. c
7. b
8. c
9. c
10. e

EXERCISE 5B

1. c
2. d
3. c
4. a
5. a
6. c

EXERCISE 5C

1. microcosm
2. expletive
3. attenuate
4. microbe(s)
5. minutiae
6. satiate(d)

LESSON 6

EXERCISE 6A

1. e
2. a
3. a
4. a
5. b
6. a
7. a

EXERCISE 6B

1. b
2. b
3. c
4. b

EXERCISE 6C

1. magnate
2. polygamous
3. polygon
4. copious
5. macrocosm
6. megalomania
7. magnanimous(ly)

REVIEW EXERCISES FOR LESSONS 5 AND 6

EXERCISE 1

1. e
2. e
3. *tenuare,* make thin
4. plenty
5. *magnus, megas*

EXERCISE 2

3. a. magnates . . . expletives . . . tenuous
3. b. minutiae . . . copious
3. c. minuscule . . . microcosm

LESSON 7

EXERCISE 7A
1. d
2. a
3. a
4. d
5. e
6. e

EXERCISE 7B
1. c
2. a
3. a
4. c
5. d
6. d

EXERCISE 7C
1. predestine
2. premonition
3. antebellum
4. precept(s)
5. anterior
6. avant-garde
7. pretentious
8. antecedent(s)
9. preempt(ed)

LESSON 8

EXERCISE 8A
1. d
2. b
3. a
4. b
5. e
6. a

EXERCISE 8B
1. c
2. c
3. d
4. c
5. b

EXERCISE 8C
1. posterior
2. posterity
3. posthumous
4. primate(s)
5. prime
6. premier(s)

REVIEW EXERCISES FOR LESSONS 7 AND 8
1. *primus*, first
2. *pre, ante*
3. first book; first school; an action that must come first
4. d
5. b

LESSON 9

EXERCISE 9A

1. a
2. b
3. d
4. a
5. c
6. e
7. d
8. d
9. d
10. e

EXERCISE 9B

1. a
2. b
3. b
4. d
5. c

EXERCISE 9C

1. artisan(s)
2. depict(ed)
3. parody
4. artifact(s)
5. ode
6. artifice
7. Pictograph(s)

LESSON 10

EXERCISE 10A

1. c
2. e
3. d
4. a
5. b

EXERCISE 10B

1. d
2. c
3. d
4. b
5. c
6. d
7. c
8. a
9. b

REVIEW EXERCISES FOR LESSONS 9 AND 10

EXERCISE 1

1. b
2. d
3. b
4. a
5. c

EXERCISE 2

1. a. (could) mollify (the children)
   b. an efficacious (remedy)
   c. incantations
   d. (so) artless . . . (their) pretext
   e. (If you) recant

LESSON 11

EXERCISE 11A

1. a
2. c
3. c
4. a
5. c
6. a
7. b
8. e

EXERCISE 11B

1. a
2. c
3. c
4. b

EXERCISE 11C

1. episode(s)
2. transitory or transient
3. exodus
4. transitive
5. obituary
6. ambience

LESSON 12

EXERCISE 12A

1. c
2. a
3. c
4. d
5. a
6. c
7. c
8. e

EXERCISE 12B

1. d
2. c
3. b
4. b
5. b

EXERCISE 12C

1. advent
2. circumvent
3. deviate
4. covene(d)
5. itinerary
6. impervious

REVIEW EXERCISES FOR LESSONS 11 AND 12

1. a
2. d
3. e
4. a
5. c
6. journey
7. to come, to go

LESSON 13

EXERCISE 13A
1. b
2. b
3. d
4. e
5. b
6. b
7. d

EXERCISE 13B
1. b
2. d
3. a
4. b
5. a
6. c

EXERCISE 13C
1. conglomeration
2. celerity
3. interjection
4. abject
5. accelerate
6. concur

LESSON 14

EXERCISE 14A
1. d
2. d
3. a
4. e
5. a
6. d

EXERCISE 14B
1. c
2. d
3. a
4. c
5. d

EXERCISE 14C
1. desultory
2. prevalent
3. resilient
4. salient
5. voluble

REVIEW EXERCISES FOR LESSONS 13 AND 14
1. b
2. c
3. e
4. d
5. b

LESSON 15

EXERCISE 15A
1. d
2. b
3. c
4. e
5. c

EXERCISE 15B
1. c
2. d
3. b
4. a

EXERCISE 15C
1. capricious
2. equestrian(s)
3. apiary
4. equine
5. canine(s)
6. caper(s) or caprice(s)

LESSON 16

EXERCISE 16A
1. a
2. d
3. b
4. e
5. d
6. a
7. c

EXERCISE 16B
1. b
2. c
3. d
4. d
5. b
6. c

EXERCISE 16C
1. feline
2. Piscine
3. zoology

REVIEW EXERCISES FOR LESSONS 15 AND 16
1. g
2. c
3. h
4. a
5. i
6. b
7. e
8. j
9. f
10. d